UNDERSTANDING RAWLS

UNDERSTANDING RAWLS

A Reconstruction and Critique of
A THEORY OF JUSTICE

by Robert Paul Wolff

PRINCETON UNIVERSITY PRESS
PRINCETON, NEW JERSEY

Copyright © 1977 by Princeton University Press
Published by Princeton University Press, Princeton, New Jersey
In the United Kingdom: Princeton University Press,
Guildford, Surrey

All Rights Reserved

Library of Congress Cataloging in Publication Data will
be found on the last printed page of this book

Published with the aid of The Paul Mellon Fund at
Princeton University Press

This book has been composed in VIP Caledonia

Printed in the United States of America
by Princeton University Press, Princeton, New Jersey

To the memory of
Charlotte Ornstein Wolff
1900–1975

BOOKS BY ROBERT PAUL WOLFF

Kant's Theory of Mental Activity (1963)
Political Man and Social Man (editor, 1965)
A Critique of Pure Tolerance (with Barrington Moore, Jr., and Herbert Marcuse, 1965)
Kant: A Collection of Critical Essays (editor, 1967)
The Poverty of Liberalism (1968)
Kant's Groundwork: Text and Commentary (editor, 1968)
The Essential Hume (editor, 1969)
The Ideal of the University (1969)
Ten Great Works of Philosophy (editor, 1969)
In Defense of Anarchism (1970)
Philosophy: A Modern Encounter (1971)
The Rule of Law (editor, 1971)
Styles of Political Action in America (editor, 1972)
1984 Revisited: Prospects for American Politics (editor, 1973)
The Autonomy of Reason: A Commentary on Kant's Groundwork of the Metaphysics of Morals (1973)
About Philosophy (1975)

Contents

Preface

THIS book grows out of my efforts to make *A Theory of Justice* clear to myself and my students in a graduate course in political philosophy at the University of Massachusetts at Amherst. When I sat down to prepare my lectures on John Rawls's philosophy, in the fall of 1975, I felt a need to write out my remarks so that I could keep my thoughts in order. The result was the manuscript from which the present book has come.

A number of students offered insights, arguments, objections, and suggestions from which I have benefited. Judith Decew, in her term paper, first called my attention to the argument by John Harsanyi about maximin and probability assignments, which I have summarized in a note to Section XV. Peter Markie helped me to understand some of the logical differences between the first and final forms of Rawls's bargaining game. And Jim Lane and Mark Richard, in the course of a game theory study group that met throughout the spring of 1976, enormously improved my grasp of the logical structure of the bargaining game under the veil of ignorance.

As has now become my habit, as well as my pleasure, I consulted my good friend and colleague, Professor Robert J. Ackermann, on a number of technical matters that threatened to get beyond me.

Only those who are familiar with the literary criticism of my wife, Professor Cynthia Griffin Wolff, will recognize how much my own work has been influenced by hers. Over many years, she has deepened and complicated my understanding both of the human psyche and of the written word. In the midst of preparing her most recent book for publication, she took time to read carefully through this manuscript. The result was the elimination of a number of egregious blunders and infelicities. This essay is written, as is all my philosophy, for her.

Northampton
May 1976

PART ONE
INTRODUCTION

I

Introductory Remarks

A THEORY OF JUSTICE, by John Rawls, is an important book, but it is also a puzzling book. It is extremely long, and parts of it move very slowly. Rawls shifts repeatedly from the most sophisticated deployment of the formal models of economics and mathematics to discussions of outdated topics, materials, and references drawn from the ideal utilitarian, intuitionist, and empirical psychological schools of English thought that flourished in the late nineteenth and early twentieth centuries. The book gives every evidence of having been elaborately cross-referenced, unified, and synthesized, as though each element of the argument had been weighed in relation to each other; yet there are numerous serious inconsistencies and unclarities that make it appear that Rawls could not make up his mind on some quite fundamental questions. The logical status of the claims in the book never becomes entirely clear, despite Rawls's manifest concern with matters of that sort. In many places, he seems simply to admit that he has adjusted his premises to make them yield the conclusions he desires; yet elsewhere, from the first pages to the last, he claims to have proved, or at least to have sketched the proof of, a "theorem" of some sort.

The importance of Rawls's work, and also its unclarity, is attested by the flood of comments that have appeared in the half-decade since its publication. Philosophers, economists, and political scientists have all sought to get a handhold on the book, with results sometimes like those of the blind men and the elephant.[1] I think a good deal of sense can be made of Rawls's book, though in the end I do not think his claims can be sustained. But in order to get at that sense, we must adopt a somewhat unorthodox exegetical stance.

Briefly, I propose to read *A Theory of Justice* not as a single piece of philosophical argument to be tested and accepted or rejected whole, but as a complex, many-layered record of at least twenty years of philosophical growth and development. I shall argue that Rawls began with a simple, coherent, comprehensible problem and a brilliant idea for its solution. His original intention must have been to write a book very much like Kenneth Arrow's *Social Choice and Individual Values*, which would present the solution to his problem as a formal theorem of enormous power and significance. The idea turned out not to work, although it was nonetheless an idea of great originality. The labyrinthine complexities of *A Theory of Justice* are the consequences of at least three stages in the development of Rawls's thought, in each of which he complicated his theory to meet objections others had raised to earlier versions, or which he himself perceived. At one key point in this development—roughly when he introduced the notion of a "veil of ignorance"—Rawls saw a way to connect up his argument with a quite distinct tradition of moral and political theory, and this fact clearly encouraged him to think that the revised and complicated version was superior to the original. As the cautions, qualifications, and complications were added

---

[1] Several bibliographies of books and articles on Rawls have already appeared, though each is out of date shortly after its publication. Readers interested in exploring the literature will get some assistance from a brief annotated bibliography at the end of this essay. Where my remarks echo those of other writers, I have tried to indicate that fact in the text.

to the theory, it grew less plausible intuitively, and very much less like a "theorem" of the sort Rawls had set out to prove. Yet the language of his book shows that he never gave up the dream, using to the end such terms as "proof," "theorem," and "theory."

My historical reconstruction of the development of Rawls's theory is not entirely speculative, of course. What I shall be calling the first form of the model was set forth in his essay entitled "Justice as Fairness," which appeared in the *Philosophical Review* in 1958 and has been often reprinted.[2] A much-altered version of the theory, corresponding roughly to what I call the second form of the model, was offered in Rawls's 1967 article, "Distributive Justice," which appeared as an original essay in the third series of Laslett and Runciman's *Philosophy, Politics, and Society*. These two essays, taken together with the final version of *A Theory of Justice*, constitute considerable evidence of the development of Rawls's thought.

Nevertheless, the principal argument for the reconstruction I shall develop in this essay is its success in helping us to understand a number of elements in the final theory whose presence and precise role are otherwise simply baffling. In terms of the reconstruction, we shall be able to understand why the participants in the original position are assumed, rather arbitrarily, to be free of envy; why a difficult and controversial theory of primary goods must be posited; why a veil of ignorance is necessary, and why it must be supposed not to blot out a knowledge of what Rawls rather vaguely calls the basic facts of society and moral psychology; why the first principle of justice is asserted to take priority over the sec-

[2] I shall refer to it as it was reprinted in *Philosophy, Politics, and Society*, edited by Peter Laslett and W. G. Runciman (Barnes & Noble, Inc., 1962) second series.

ond; and why the participants in the original position somewhat unaccountably eschew the principle of insufficient reason for the highly controversial maximin principle of decision making under uncertainty.

In the development of my reconstruction, before I reach the point at which I state my own criticisms of the theory, I shall be focusing attention on elements of the various "models" which Rawls himself has subsequently altered or entirely given up; and I shall either ignore or rather summarily dismiss elements of the final theory on which Rawls explicitly places great weight. This style of criticism and interpretation raises some very difficult questions of philosophical method, and it might be best to lay my cards on the table in the opening pages of this essay, so that readers can better judge what follows. I hope at the same time to be able to explain why I believe that this essay can, at one and the same time, be of use and of interest both to the beginning student of Rawls who is seeking guidance in mastering A Theory of Justice and to the scholar or critic who wishes to come to some judgment of its lasting importance and validity.

There are among contemporary American philosophers two, contrary conceptions of how philosophy ought to be done, what the marks are of good philosophy, and how one ought to judge the worth, positively or negatively, of philosophical theses and arguments. Although both conceptions are held, in various forms and to varying degrees, by philosophers who would be described as "analytic" in their methodology and orientation, they find expression in very different sorts of philosophical writing. One view is that much of the value of a philosophical position consists in the precision, detail, and completeness with which it is elaborated. Philosophers of this persuasion devote a great deal of energy and imagination to defending their claims against objections, particularly as those objections take the form of counterexamples to general theses that have been advanced. The performative character of Descartes's *cogito*, or Kant's notion of a transcendental argument, is subjected to anatomical dissection, with successive formulations and reformulations of the same central idea being proposed, criticized, revised, and criticized anew. The model for philosophical work of this sort is formal logic, where a theorem is invalidated by a single counterexample, no matter how bizarre or peripheral. The proponents of this methodological position, I think it fair to say, are likely to prefer the full-scale, incredibly detailed final version of Rawls's theory, as it is laid out in *A Theory of Justice*, to the relatively brief sketches of it that appeared in the earlier articles.

The opposed conception of philosophy, which I espouse, is that the real value of a philosophical position lies almost entirely in the depth, the penetration, and the power of its central insight. In the *Critique of Pure Reason*, for example, Kant develops his strategy of defending the fundamental claims of science and mathematics against skeptical attack by exhibiting them as grounded in the possibility of consciousness in general. Nothing genuinely new and important has been added by the countless philosophers who have classified, catalogued, criticized, and multiplied "transcendental arguments" in the journals.

A new philosophical idea, needless to say, may be quite technical. Like the idea at the heart of a mathematical proof, it may require considerable background and sophistication to be understood. But, like a really original idea in mathematics, it can usually be grasped in one single act of thought. The central theses of the *Critique of Pure Reason* are fundamentally simple—not easy to understand, but not elaborately complicated in

7

their detail. I believe that philosophy advances by quantum leaps, as genuinely new insights are achieved; it does not inch forward step by step, pulled along by the yeoman labor of countless journeymen thinkers.

What is the implication of these remarks for this essay? Well, if you hold the first conception of philosophy, then a book on Rawls must be *either* elementary, introductory, and expository, *or else* advanced, detailed, and critical. A "contribution to scholarship" will consist of criticism of particular points in Rawls, an understanding of which presupposes that one already has a firm grasp of the text. But if you agree with me in holding the second conception of philosophy, then you will believe that it is at least possible to write an essay on Rawls that is at one and the same time an aid to understanding for the intelligent beginning student and also a genuine philosophical contribution to scholarship in the field. To accomplish this, we shall have to grasp the core insight or idea of *A Theory of Justice*, lay it bare in a clear manner, and then expose its strengths and weaknesses as a fundamental idea, independently of the particularities in which it is nested. If we are successful, it will then be possible to understand those particularities as variations upon the central idea, defenses of it against possible attacks, and so forth.

The order of my exposition will be as follows. In the remaining two sections of Part One, I shall sketch the original problem, or complex of problems, that Rawls faced when he began the development of his theory. Then I shall state what I take to be the central idea, or key, of Rawls's work, and indicate why I think that it is an original, important, and powerful philosophical idea.

In Part Two, I shall unfold the development of Rawls's theory, from its first relatively simple form in the 1958 article, "Justice as Fairness," to the final baroque com-

plexity of *A Theory of Justice*. I shall proceed dialecti-
cally, by stating the first form of Rawls's model, subjecting it to criticism, moving on to the second, revised form
of the model, subjecting it in turn to criticism, and then
spelling out the elements of the full-scale form of the
model as it appears in the book. The purpose of this
mode of exposition is to show that many of the elements
of the final theory were introduced not because of their
intrinsic philosophical merit, but rather as devices for
meeting actual or possible objections. A particularly important complication in the final model, the so-called
"priority of liberty," will then be factored into the account, and Part Two will be brought to a close with a
brief discussion of some secondary elaborations and
complications that Rawls adds to the model in its official
form.

Part Three of this essay is devoted to an extended discussion of the relation between Rawls and Kant, with
particular attention to Rawls's own view of that relationship. As we shall see, Rawls is wrong about the connec-
tions between his political philosophy and Kant's moral
theory, but he is quite correct in insisting on the significance of the comparison.

The first three parts of this essay are essentially recon-
structive and expository, despite the presence of a considerable body of critical argument. Part Four, building
on the analysis of the preceding sections, presents my
own substantive critique of Rawls's theory. Some of my
remarks repeat the objections of other scholars, and I
shall try through footnote references to give the reader
some guidance to existing critical literature; certain of
my criticisms are, I believe, original, although the response to Rawls has been so rapid and widespread that I
cannot be certain that I have not been anticipated. The
aim of the discussion in Part Four will be to show that

Rawls's model is ultimately unsatisfactory, despite the rather inventive adjustments by which he seeks to shore it up. Since Rawls begins his book with some methodological remarks concerning what he calls "reflective equilibrium," I conclude Part Four with a discussion of the logical status of the argument of *A Theory of Justice*.

Were I to close my discussion at that point, the most important question of all would remain: what are we to make of Rawls's theory of justice? If I am right that the value of a philosopher's work lies in the power and fecundity of its core insight, rather than in the detail of its exposition, then I can scarcely evade the responsibility to come to some judgment of the idea that I perceive at the heart of Rawls's philosophy. I believe that Rawls's reliance on certain formal models of analysis drawn from the theory of rational choice is fundamentally wrong, that his use of the concepts and models of utility theory, welfare economics, and game theory, which is at the very heart of his enterprise, is the wrong way to deal with the normative and explanatory problems of social theory. In the final part of this essay, I shall elaborate on this claim and do my best to make it plausible.

II

The Problem

THE problem with which Rawls begins is the impasse in Anglo-American ethical theory at about the beginning of the 1950s. If we leave to one side emotivism in any of its various forms, the major cognitivist schools of ethical theory were utilitarianism and intuitionism. Each of these traditions has strengths, from Rawls's point of view, but each also has fatal weaknesses. Rawls revives a version of the theory of the social contract as a way of discovering a *via media* between utilitarianism and intuitionism.

The principal strengths of utilitarianism are, first, its straightforward assertion of the fundamental value of human happiness and, second, its constructive character—its enunciation, that is to say, of a rule or procedure by which ethical questions are to be answered and ethical disputes resolved. A secondary merit of utilitarianism, both for its originators and for Rawls, is its suitability as a principle for the settling of questions of social policy. The two most obvious weaknesses of utilitarianism are its inability to explain how rationally self-interested pleasure-maximizers are to be led to substitute the general happiness for their own as the object of their actions and the manifestly counterintuitive, sometimes genuinely abhorrent implications of its fundamental principle. The examples of this second failing are well-known, of course, but it is worth remembering that the most striking counterinstances to the principle of utility arise precisely in connection with issues of procedural or substantive justice.

As a moral theory, intuitionism is methodologically inferior to utilitarianism. It simply asserts, flatly and without proof, that each of us has a power of "moral intuition," called "rational" by intuitionists but exhibiting no structure of practical reasoning, whereby we can directly apprehend the obligatoriness of particular acts.[3] Even the addition by W. D. Ross of the notion of prima facie obligation fails to transform intuitionism into a theory of moral reasoning, for when we are called on to estimate the relative weights of conflicting prima facie duties, we must once again rely solely on intuition. But while intuitionism is weak as an account of practical reasoning, it is strong in two respects that are clearly important to Rawls. First, it defines the right independently of the good, and so makes rightness a fundamental, irreducibly moral notion; second, it takes over from Kant the doctrine of the inviolability and dignity of moral personality, and thereby decisively rejects the utilitarian tendency to view human beings as nothing more than pleasure-containers, to be filled or emptied like so many water jugs.

In this dispute, both Rawls's sympathies and his antipathies are evenly divided. Morally, he is clearly more comfortable with the intuitionists than with the utilitarians; but methodologically his heart is with the utilitarians, and with the neo-classical economists who took utilitarianism as the moral foundation of their elegant theoretical constructions. Utilitarianism, in even its most sophisticated and complicated versions, countenances the sacrifice of some persons to the happiness of others. As Rawls argues in a number of sections of his book, it treats individual human beings as so many dimensions along which happiness can be distributed,

---

[3] See, for example, W. D. Ross, *The Right and The Good*, or H. A. Prichard, *Moral Obligation*.

rather than as autonomous moral agents each independently pursuing a freely chosen course of action with reason and dignity. But intuitionism is a mere expression of conviction, a confession of the failure of practical reason. To even the most decent and well-intentioned moral agent who wonders what he should do or perceives a conflict between two acknowledged obligations, the intuitionist can only say, consult your intuitions. If my intuitions differ from those of the intuitionist, he can offer literally no argument to persuade me, no matter how willing I am to listen.

With this impasse as his starting point, Rawls defines his problem. Let me begin, we can imagine him thinking, with as narrow and morally neutral a conception of rational agency as can plausibly be drawn—a conception that should be acceptable to utilitarians and intuitionists alike. (Let me suppose that men seek happiness) but let me not jump to the conclusion that happiness is The Good, and most certainly let me not slip into the supposition that the happiness of all is The Good for all. Clearly, the bare notion of rational agency is insufficient for a rationally defended morality, but is there anything that can be added to these elements, short of the mere positing of substantive moral claims, that will yield a rational argument for a moral principle that is constructive, that conforms to, or at least does not deviate wildly from, our strongest moral convictions, that gives an independent logical status to the notion of the right, and that takes the inviolability and dignity of moral personality as fundamental?

(At this point Rawls turns to a third tradition, not strictly in moral or social philosophy but rather in political theory: the tradition of the social contract) Historically, the device of the social contract has been invoked for the purpose of explaining or justifying the authority of the state. It belongs to the longer tradition of debates about the nature and locus of sovereignty, and it concerns itself therefore with the formal problems of the nature and legitimacy of authority rather than with substantive problems of social policy and distributive justice. The common theme in the various contract theories is the claim that sovereignty resides originally in individuals, so that both the assembling or aggregating of it into a unity and the transferring of it to a bearer who will exercise it require a collective (and usually unanimous) agreement of the original sovereignty-holders.

From the standpoint of moral theory, there are really two contractarian traditions. The first, represented by Locke, assumes a moral theory as one of the premises of the argument concerning the contract. In Locke's *Second Treatise*, a full-scale moral theory of natural rights and the law of nature is simply posited, roughly along intuitionist lines. The substance and validity of the contract is made by Locke to rest on that theory, which tells him not only why the state has a right to rule and what its rightful purposes are but also what the limits are of its authority and under what conditions individuals have the right to overthrow it.

The second contractarian tradition derives from Rousseau. It too begins with a state of nature and a theory of human nature, but it asserts (however paradoxically) that the entry into civil society by means of a social contract works a moral transformation on the original contractors. Not merely the substance, but the form, of men's moral reasoning is changed by the contract. Prior to agreement, each individual has what Rousseau calls a "private will." But upon entering the compact, each individual acquires a general will, or rather acquires the opportunity for the first time to have or exercise a general will. (The transformation is moral, not psychological.) The most

14

benevolent person imaginable could not, in a state of nature, have a general will, any more than a group of coworkers could, in the absence of a legal system, constitute themselves a limited liability corporation.

Rawls proposes to advance beyond the point at which the moral theories of utilitarianism and intuitionism have bogged down by invoking a version of the theory of the social contract in its Rousseauean form. By so doing, he will unite moral and social philosophy in a way more reminiscent of Plato than of Locke or Bentham or Mill. And, he hopes, he will be able to formulate a fundamental principle of moral and social theory that is constructive, rational, attentive both to the good of human happiness and to the dignity of moral personality, and for which an argument can be given that has some hope of persuading those who are not already convinced.

III

The Key

AT this point, Rawls had an idea. It was, I venture to say, one of the loveliest ideas in the history of social and political theory.[4] Although Rawls's problem grew out of the history of moral philosophy, and even in the 1950s had a somewhat antique flavor, with its elaborate concern about the rather peculiar doctrine of intuitionism, his idea was, as chess players would say, hyper-modern. Rawls proposed to construct a formal model of a society of rationally self-interested individuals, whom he would imagine to be engaged in what the modern theory of rational choice calls a *bargaining game*. His intuition was that if he constituted the bargaining game along the lines suggested by the contractarian tradition of political theory—if, that is to say, he posited a group of individuals whose nature and motives were those usually assumed in contract theory—then with a single additional quasi-formal, substantively empty constraint, he could prove, as a formal theorem in the theory of rational choice, that *the* solution to the bargaining game was a moral principle having the characteristics of constructivity, coherence with our settled moral convictions, and rationality, and making an independent place for the notion of the right while acknowledging the dignity and worth of moral personality. The

---

[4] It may seem odd to describe a philosophical idea as "lovely," but mathematicians are accustomed to applying terms of aesthetic evaluation to abstract ideas, and Rawls's theory is, in my judgment, a simple, elegant, formal maneuver, embedded in and nearly obscured by an enormous quantity of substantive exemplification.

constraint Rawls hit upon was so minimal, so natural, so manifestly a constraint under which any person would consent to operate insofar as he made any pretensions at all to having a morality, that Rawls would, if he could prove his theorem, be in a position to say to a reader:

If you are a rationally self-interested agent, and if you are to have a morality at all, then you must acknowledge as binding upon you the moral principle I shall enunciate.

Not surprisingly, this is almost exactly the claim made by Immanuel Kant for his Categorical Imperative in the *Groundwork of the Metaphysic of Morals*.

Rawls's bargaining game is a non-zero-sum cooperative game, whose aim is for the players to arrive at unanimous agreement on a set of principles that will henceforth serve as the criteria for evaluating the institutions or practices within which the players interact.[5] The game consists of a series of proposals made by each player in turn for consideration by all the rest, and play terminates when there is unanimous agreement on a single set of principles. The players are assumed to be rationally self-interested, as in all such games, but they are assumed also to operate under a single additional constraint not deducible from the definition of rational self-interest: it is posited that once they have agreed upon a set of principles, chosen though they have been on the basis of a calculation of self-interest, they will abide by those principles in all future cases, including those in which—even taking all side and long-term effects into account—it is not in their self-interest so to abide. As Rawls says in "Justice as Fairness," "having a

[5] For an explanation of some of the terminology of game theory, and a discussion of certain unclarities in Rawls's characterization of the bargaining game, see the technical appendix to Section V, below, and also Section XV.

17

morality is analogous to having made a firm commitment in advance; for one must acknowledge the principles of morality even when to one's disadvantage." The solution proposed by Rawls to this bargaining game is, of course, the now-famous Two Principles of Justice.

In a moment, we shall take a close look at Rawls's first characterization of the bargaining game and its solution—what I shall be calling the First Form of the Model. But it is worth pausing for a bit to reflect on the elegance and beauty of this idea. It is the central idea of Rawls's philosophy, and through all the transformations and elaborations of the theory, it persists as the key to his thought. The real force of the idea can be appreciated if we remind ourselves of some facts about the history and development of rational moral theory.

In the opening paragraphs of the *Groundwork of the Metaphysic of Morals*, Kant writes that "all rational knowledge is either *material* and concerned with some object, or *formal* and concerned solely with the form of understanding and reason themselves—with the universal rules of thinking as such without regard to differences of objects."[6] In its theoretical activities, man's reason is guided by the laws of logic—by the law of contradiction, the rules of syllogistic inference, and so forth. These laws are purely formal; they deal with the *form* of our assertions (such as "All *A* are *B*," or "If *p* then *q*"). They say nothing about the *matter* or content of knowledge-claims (such as whether this particular sort of *A* really is a *B*). The crucial fact about logic, as every beginning student learns, is that while the formal laws of reasoning can rule

[6] *Kants Werke*, Ak. iv, 387. The translation is by H. J. Paton. For a discussion of the *Groundwork*, and a defense of the interpretation of Kant's philosophy adopted in this essay, see my *The Autonomy of Reason: A Commentary on Kant's Groundwork of the Metaphysic of Morals* (Harper & Row, 1973).

out certain propositions as self-contradictory merely by virtue of their form, and hence as surely false, those laws cannot rule *in* just those propositions whose content makes them true. "All men are immortal" is just as good as "All men are mortal," so far as logic is concerned.

In ethics, or what Kant called the practical employment of reason, it is possible to find purely formal laws to which all moral principles must conform, although, as we might expect, they tend to be more controversial than the law of contradiction or the rules of inference. One such law is the law of efficiency or prudence, which says, to put it about as simple-mindedly as possible: whatever you do, do it as cheaply as you can, however you count costs. A rule like this has some bite, just as the law of contradiction does. If I want to get from New York to San Francisco for as little money as possible, so long as I can complete the trip in twenty-four hours, then the law of prudence tells me to buy a tourist-class rather than a first-class plane ticket. But, of course, neither the law of prudence *nor any other purely formal law of practical reason* can tell me whether I ought to go to San Francisco! And there's the rub. When it comes to the ends, or goals, or purposes of my action, reason alone seems not to be able to guide me.

Kant thought that the failure to provide some philosophical justification for the matter or content of theoretical reason would reduce us to the barren skepticism of David Hume. The analogous failure in ethics, he thought, would leave us with nothing more than the merely formal principles of efficiency or prudence. We would have no objective rational grounds for choosing one system of ends or goals rather than another, and we would therefore possess nothing resembling substantive, objective moral principles. So, he concluded, we would either be forced to retreat to the subjectivity of pru-

19

dence, as utilitarianism, for all its efforts to the contrary, ultimately does; or else we would, in desperation, simply have to posit substantive objective moral principles without a suggestion of rational argument, as does intuitionism. In the *Groundwork*, Kant struggled to escape this dilemma by attempting the impossible feat of deducing substantive conclusions from purely formal premises.

The brilliance of Rawls's idea lies in its promise of a way out of the impasse to which Kant had brought moral theory, an impasse that, as we have already seen, still blocked moral philosophers almost two centuries later. Through the device of a bargaining game, Rawls hopes to derive substantive principles from premises that, though not purely formal, are not manifestly material either. The constraint of commitment is a procedural constraint, a quasi-formal premise making no reference to specific ends at which the players in the bargaining game must aim. The constraint merely says, "You must be willing, once you have arrived at a satisfactory principle, to commit yourselves to it for all time, no matter what." No limits are placed on *what* principle shall be adopted, nor are the players required to adopt their principle for "ethical" rather than self-interested reasons.

Even if Rawls's theorem can be established, the self-interested moral skeptic may still decline to make a once-and-for-all commitment, even to a principle chosen from self-interest. Fidelity to principle is not, after all, deducible from bare formal rationality, at least not without some rather powerful metaphysical assumptions about the timeless character of the moral agent (*qua noumenon*, in Kant's language). But Rawls will be able to resolve the dispute between the utilitarian and the intuitionist, both of whom acknowledge the bindingness of principles, and he will be able to do a good deal more

20

besides. He will, by this maneuver, have achieved for his principles of justice the same sort of conditionally a priori status that Kant claimed for the system of principles of pure understanding in the *Critique of Pure Reason*.[7]

[7] For an extended discussion of the relationship between Rawls and Kant, see Part Three. See also, *The Autonomy of Reason*, Conclusion.

PART TWO
THE DEVELOPMENT OF THE THEORY

IV

The First Form of the Model

IN its first form, Rawls's model is simple, clear, elegant, and—as we shall see—subject to devastating objections. Despite its shortcomings, however, the first form of the model is, I will argue, the real foundation on which all the rest of Rawls's theory is constructed. I shall therefore subject it to rather close scrutiny.[8]

Rawls announces that his concern is with justice "as a virtue of social institutions, or what I shall call practices" (132). A practice is defined as "any form of activity specified by a system of rules which define offices, roles, moves, penalties, defences, and so on, and which give the activity its structure" (132 note). The notion of a practice is central to the model, for the bargaining game is a game whose outcome or solution is an agreement on the principles to be used in determining whether practices are acceptable—whether they are, in their structure rather than merely in their implementation, "just." Several things are clear in this early conception of a practice that become rather blurry later on. First, each practice must be defined by its rules and roles, independently of the rewards or burdens assigned to the various roles. If this were not so, it would be impossible to require of a given practice, as Rawls does two pages later,

[8] In this section and the next, I shall deal principally with the 1958 essay, "Justice as Fairness." Page references in parentheses are to the Laslett and Runciman reprint. Some of what I say about this version of Rawls's theory is drawn from my article, "A Refutation of Rawls's Theorem on Justice," *J. Phil.*, 63 (March 31, 1966), pp. 179–90.

that "the representative man in every office or position defined by the practice, when he views it as a going concern, must find it reasonable to prefer his condition and prospects with the inequality to what they would be under the practice [the *same* practice, presumably] without it" (135). Now, for marginal variations in payoffs this conception of the relation between a practice and its pattern of rewards is plausible. A practice or institution such as a hospital is manifestly the *same* practice or institution even if a slight shift in compensation is made from the chiefs of service to the interns, or from the head nurse to the floor nurses. But if major redistributions are considered, such that, say, the highly paid chief of surgery is reduced in pay to the level of an orderly while maintenance workers are advanced in pay above staff doctors, it is not at all clear whether we would or could consider the two arrangements as instantiations of the *same* practice with different payoffs. In the first place, the payoffs assigned to a role are in some sense a part of that role; and in the second place, significant collateral factors such as power and authority relationships, patterns of deference, and modes of functional coordination would be altered by more than marginal rearrangements of payoffs. (Later on, Rawls shifts his attention from such small-scale practices, on what economists call the micro level, to the fundamental system of social and economic institutions in a society as a whole, corresponding to the macro level of analysis in economics) But this raises a new problem, one that had been nicely handled by the early, simpler conception of a practice.

Rawls's theory speaks of the expectations of *representative* men. In the first model, each representative man must believe that an unequal distribution works to his advantage. In the second and subsequent models, the so-called "difference principle" is substituted, according to which the least advantaged representative man must expect inequalities to work for his benefit. But in either case, it is assumed that we are able to identify the various representative men. Now, in the original conception of practices, representative men are clearly identified by the rules of the practice, in a manner analogous to—or perhaps even identical to—the way in which players are identified by the rules of a game. In the game of baseball, for example, it is clear from the rules that there are nine players on each side (not counting pinch hitters, relief pitchers, managers, coaches, and so forth). If a dispute were to arise over the fairness of the game of baseball, no credence would be given to a tricky argument designed to show that the game met Rawls's difference principle so long as we construed the rules as defining four "representative men," namely outfielder, infielder, pitcher, and catcher. But when we ask which individuals in an industrial society are to be construed as constituting the "least advantaged group," it is not at all obvious whether we are to focus on the working class as a whole, or on unskilled workers, or on black, unskilled women, or whatever. The most natural extension of Rawls's notion of a practice to an entire society would be a functionalist Marxian analysis in terms of the structure of production and the social relationships of production, but Rawls himself tends to speak the language of liberal American sociology, which substitutes a scale of socioeconomic status for the concept of economic class. Once this move has been made, cut-off points become conventional rather than objective, and it is not surprising to find Rawls flirting with the notion of chain-connectedness as a way of finessing these difficulties.

Having sketched the notion of a practice, Rawls now develops the elements of his bargaining game. We are to imagine a society of rational agents among whom a sys-

27

tem of practices is already established. The members of the society have the following characteristics:

1. They make decisions on the basis of enlightened self-interest, and are capable both of discovering their own preferences and of evaluating with reasonable success the consequences of their and others' actions.[9]

2. They have roughly similar needs and interests, or at least needs and interests that make self-interested cooperation among them rational.

3. They are "sufficiently equal in power and ability to guarantee that in normal circumstances none is able to dominate the others" (138).

4. They are not envious; which is to say, "the bare knowledge or perception of the difference between their condition and that of others is not, within limits and in itself, a source of great dissatisfaction" (137).

Condition 1 is the classical assumption of rational self-interest with which both welfare economics and game theory begin. Condition 2 guarantees that the individuals will continue to engage in practices, since, if cooperation is contrary to the interests of a significant number, the society will disintegrate either into the war of all against all or into a mere atomized multiplicity of independent units. Condition 3 guarantees that in con-

[9] Since Rawls intends to rely, at this point, on the sort of unanimity quasi-ordering usually associated with the name of Pareto, he assumes only ordinal preference. However, in light of the calculations of "reasonable expectation" that his representative men are to make, it would appear that some conception of cardinal utility will be called for. In the final version of the model, when the veil of ignorance has been lowered, Rawls argues that the participants in the bargaining game will find it rational to adopt the maximin rule of choice under uncertainty. His reasons for this claim, as we shall see, presuppose not merely cardinal utility functions, but even utility functions with a natural zero-point. See Part Four below.

texts in which functional differentiation and integration are mutually beneficial, some mode of bargaining and exchange rather than mere domination and submission will be in everyone's rational self-interest. (Condition 2 might obtain, after all, in a master-slave situation in which one part of society, by sheer force, was able to dominate the rest and thereby to extract from it quite unfavorable terms of "cooperation," which were nevertheless superior to a total breakdown of all social practices.)

Condition 4, the "non-envy" stipulation, has given rise to a good deal of comment in the literature on Rawls. The reason for its presence, as we shall see, is that without it one cannot conveniently employ the quasi-ordering relation of unanimous preference introduced by Pareto. If individuals are assumed to have positive marginal utility for each commodity, or for some index of commodities, or for money (whichever measure Rawls chooses to use in discussing distributions to the roles defined by a practice); and if each individual prefers one distribution to another if and only if the first gives him more of each commodity, or a higher index of commodities, or more money, than the second (assuming that any other constraints and conditions are satisfied by both distributions); if, in short, in this very special and technical sense of the term, the players in the bargaining game are "non-envious"; *then* the possibility will open up, for reasons to be explained shortly, that an unequal distribution will be unanimously preferred by the players to some equal distribution at a lower level.

Later on, in *A Theory of Justice*, Rawls engages in some extremely elaborate speculative moral psychology, in part at least to lay a factual foundation for the non-envy assumption. But if I am correct, those speculations are strictly *post hoc*. The real reason for the assumption of non-envy is purely technical, and has to do with the assumptions required by the modes of quasi-economic reasoning that Rawls wishes to employ.

The key to the solution of the bargaining problem, in Rawls's view, is a fundamental fact of economic life—what I shall call the possibility of an *inequality surplus*. It sometimes happens that an unequal distribution of payoffs to the roles of a practice results in, or makes possible, a situation that is unanimously preferred to the practice without the inequality. All that is required is that the inequality should, by eliciting greater effort or a higher level of skill or whatever, increase the output of the practice sufficiently so that after the lowest paid roles are paid at the previous level of equal distribution, and all the other, better-paid roles are paid at levels sufficient to elicit the increased output, some surplus be left over with which to raise at least marginally the payoff of the lowest paid roles.

Consider, for example, a shop in which shoes are turned out by means of a productive practice in which six roles are defined. Let us suppose that there is functional differentiation but no variation in pay scales. Sixty workers occupy the six roles (not necessarily ten to each role, of course), and the net annual income of the shop before wages is $600,000. (We shall ignore profit, since, generally speaking, Rawls does also.) Each worker is paid $10,000 a year.

As things stand, the workers work at a rather leisurely rate. But we may imagine that if a faster pace of work were introduced for two of the roles, output of the shop would rise markedly. This is because the technical characteristics of the productive process create a bottleneck at those two points, such that the entire enterprise would be much more efficient if those workers could be got to work faster. Suppose that there are four workers in

30

one of the bottleneck jobs and six in the other. Suppose, furthermore, that in order to compensate those workers for the unpleasantness and greater effort of the speeded-up work—in order to get them to take those jobs—we must pay each of them $15,000 instead of $10,000. Since ten workers in all are needed for the bottleneck jobs, we shall have to find an extra $50,000 in order to run the shop in this more productive manner.

Now, there are three possibilities. The net income of the shop under the new arrangement, which by hypothesis will be more than the original $600,000, may be less than $650,000, exactly equal to $650,000, or more than $650,000. If it is less than $650,000, then we are going to have to *lower* the wages of some of the other fifty workers in order to come up with the extra $5,000 per worker required by the new system. The shop as a whole will be more productive, but there is no way that we will ever get all sixty workers to agree to the change, assuming they are rationally self-interested.

If the net income is exactly equal to $650,000, then the other fifty workers will be indifferent between the new system and the old one, for their jobs and wages will be unchanged. The ten fast workers will, by hypothesis, prefer the new system to the old, since their $15,000 salaries were assumed to be sufficient to draw them into the harder jobs, and that can only mean that they *prefer* the new work at the new wage to their old work at their old wage.

But if the net income should *exceed* $650,000, then it will be possible to give the harder working workers their increased wages and still have something left over to raise the wages of the remaining fifty workers above the previous baseline level of equal (low) pay. For example, if the net income rises to $700,000, then after the fifty regular workers are paid their $10,000 each, and the fast workers are paid $15,000 each, there will be a pot of $50,000 left over, which can be spread around among the fifty regular workers, raising their wages to $11,000 each. *That $50,000 is an inequality surplus*—it is the surplus income remaining after all the occupants of the roles of an unequally rewarded practice have been paid enough to draw them into the several roles.

And now the point of the non-envy assumption should be clear. If we were to permit the judgments of the players in our bargaining game to be influenced by "envy," then a player might so resent the $15,000 wage of his fellow worker that he would rather stick with the original equal-pay arrangement, *even though he would have to give up a $1,000 raise to do so*! If we rule out envy, however, then we can be certain that whenever an objective calculation shows that some arrangement of payoffs in a practice will produce an inequality surplus, we can conclude that there will be a possible distribution of that surplus that makes the practice *with* the inequality unanimously preferable to the same practice without the inequality.[10]

[10] If we were to attempt to formalize this discussion mathematically, some rather tricky problems would arise having to do with continuous intervals lacking lower bounds. We could get around those problems by assuming that changes in wages were possible only in discrete increments, say of $100 a year, particularly if we also assumed that the workers' utility functions were insensitive to changes in income of less than that amount. Unfortunately, we would then have to contend with the fact that indifference would not be transitive. What is more, there might be inequality surpluses too small to be spread among all the workers of a practice in discriminable amounts. However, I think we may reasonably excuse Rawls from worrying about such matters. As Aristotle said, "our discussion will be adequate if it has as much clearness as the subject-matter admits of, for precision is not to be sought for alike in all discussions, any more than in all the products of the crafts" (*Nichomachean Ethics*, I, 3).

Now let us suppose that a society of individuals conforming to this description is engaged in its established practices, and that from time to time complaints are brought by individuals against those practices. Each complaint takes the form of a claim that a certain role in a practice should receive greater rewards or have lighter duties attached to it, or that the rules governing the assignment of individuals to roles ought to be altered, or perhaps even that some new practice ought to be substituted for an existing practice. (Rawls is not concerned with complaints that the [admittedly fair] rules of a practice are being unfairly applied. That is to say, he is not interested in mere procedural justice.) Suppose further that before attempting to settle any particular claims, the society decides to select once and for all time the general principles by which all future disputes will be resolved. Rawls suggests that we imagine the members of the society to enter thereupon into the bargaining game described above. According to him, each player will reason as follows: "I want as much as I can get. Hence, I will try for a set of principles tailored to my circumstances, although I had better not be too quick to propose principles favorable to the fix I now find myself in, for I am committing myself for the entire future, whatever that may bring. But my opponents in this game are not fools, and they will of course reject such slanted proposals, if indeed they do not field some tailored to their own preferences. Clearly then I must insist on equality. They will not give me more, and I will not take less. But wait a moment. Suppose some unequal distribution can so increase the output of our practices that an inequality surplus results. In that case, if I hold out for a redistribution of that surplus that benefits every representative man, I can be certain to be absolutely better off than under a pattern of equality. Since I do not care how

33

much more my fellows gain so long as I too benefit, I will allow such inequalities as work to everyone's benefit. But I will *not* accept any unequal distribution that pushes some roles below the equality baseline in order to raise others above it. I am unwilling to take the chance that I will be stuck with that lowered role." And so the players settle on these two principles:

First, each person participating in a practice, or affected by it, has an equal right to the most extensive liberty compatible with a like liberty for all; and second, inequalities are arbitrary unless it is reasonable to expect that they will work out for everyone's advantage, and provided the positions and offices to which they attach, or from which they may be gained, are open to all.

V

A Critique of the First Form
of the Model

A T least four questions concerning the bargaining
game and these principles must be answered before
we are in a position to evaluate Rawls's claim that he has
provided us with a "sketch of a proof" (140). First, what
are the background conditions or implicit assumptions of
the bargaining game; second, how exactly are we meant
to interpret the two principles; third, do the two principles clearly and unambiguously provide an evaluation or
ranking of practices and alternative schemes of distribution within practices; and finally, would individuals
situated as Rawls assumes and engaged in such a bargaining game actually settle upon the two principles as their
unanimous choice—in short, are the two principles really the solution to the bargaining game? I shall devote
considerable time to answering these questions, despite
the fact that they are addressed to an early and discarded
version of Rawls's theory, because in my judgment most
of the subsequent development of the theory can be
traced to the difficulties raised by these questions in relation to the first form of the model.

THE BACKGROUND ASSUMPTIONS

With regard to the background assumptions or precondi-
tions of the bargaining game, several points should be
noted. The characteristics of the players and their situation cited above, with the exception of the fourth, non-

envy, constraint, constitute what Rawls refers to as the "conditions of justice." They define the circumstances in which questions of distributive justice would naturally arise. Following a tradition that goes back to Hume and beyond, Rawls assumes that in a world of overabundance, or in the absence of any mutual need for cooperation, or among creatures too aggressive to discipline themselves even for self-advantage or too empathic and altruistic to be willing to assert their own interests against others, or finally in a world in which some persons had the ability totally to dominate others and a willingness to do so, debates about justice would be moot. As Locke would put it, in such a world, either the question would not arise or it would necessarily take the form of an "appeal to heaven."

All of this is well-known and uncontroversial. But rather more important consequences flow from the character of the bargaining game itself. First of all, the game is a face-to-face bargaining confrontation, in which each proposal is made publicly and heard clearly by all participants. This feature of publicity is a stipulated element of the game, and not a sociological, political, or psychological observation about bargaining behavior. The participants are also formally equal in decision-making power by virtue of the fact that the game requires unanimity. It is simply assumed, as part of the structure of the game, that neither threats nor coercion will be used by some players to extract agreement on principles from the other. Since there are no time limits built into the game, it is a symmetrical game in which no player gains an advantage, for example, by going first, or even more importantly, by going last.[11] Each player has an equal right to participate in the discussion of alternative proposals, a

[11] See the technical appendix to this section for a discussion of the subject of symmetry.

right that follows directly from his ability to bring the bargaining to a halt by withholding his approval until he has been heard.

These various rights, usually grouped together under the heading of "political liberty," are in this first model built into the game itself; they are not made the object of deliberation within the game. Hence they take "priority" in the sense that they are presupposed by the procedures of the game. This relationship between formal, procedural elements of the game and substantive proposals for principles of distribution is a perfect model of the traditional liberal analysis of the relationship between the formal political and legal guarantees of the liberal bourgeois state and the economic arrangements or patterns of distribution arrived at by the workings of the free market. In the new welfare economics, it is assumed that the purely political liberties can be established by constitutional or political devices and that within that framework of "equal liberty" various distributive or redistributive policies can be debated. In the first version of his model, Rawls builds that traditional conception of the relationship between political liberty and economic distribution into the structure of the bargaining game. In later models, as we shall see, he significantly shifts his ground by making political liberty one of the principles chosen by the players in the game. This change, it will turn out, creates enormous logical and conceptual problems for Rawls.

THE INTERPRETATION OF THE TWO PRINCIPLES

How are we to interpret the two principles? For the sake of convenience, let us refer to the first clause, concerning the "most extensive liberty compatible with a like liberty for all," as Principle I. The requirement that inequalities work out for everyone's advantage will be referred to as Principle IIa, and the stipulation that the favored positions be open to all will be referred to as Principle IIb. Each of these components poses some problems of interpretation.

Principle I is puzzling because it refers to "liberty" rather than to wealth, or income, or rewards. The central idea behind Rawls's principles seems clear enough: the output or earnings of a practice is to be distributed equally, unless some pattern of unequal distribution can, in the manner sketched above, be made to work for everyone's benefit, and provided that everyone has a shot at the better-paid roles. In order to guarantee simple efficiency—to guarantee that the practice be near its "production frontier"—Rawls stipulates the most *extensive* liberty compatible with a like liberty for all. Otherwise, the principle would fail to move us from an equal distribution at a low level of payoff, in which some portion of the total product of the practice was simply wasted, to a position of higher equal payoff, in which the entire product was distributed. Since the latter would be unanimously preferred to the former, rationally self-interested players would insist that it be achieved whenever possible.

But if this is Rawls's meaning, why does he speak of "equal liberty"? In light of the subsequent revision of his two principles and the introduction of the rule of the priority of liberty, it would be natural to interpret him here as intending to distinguish between questions of political liberty and questions of economic distribution. The confusion could then be put down to a simple lapse in formulation. But there are two reasons for rejecting this construction, both in my judgment decisive. First of all, when Rawls himself glosses the second principle, he makes it clear that he intends it as a qualification on the first principle of equality, rather than as a separate principle addressing a different subject. He says: "The second principle defines what sorts of inequalities are permissible; it specifies how the presumption laid down by the first principle may be put aside" (135). Notice: Rawls does not say that the second principle specifies the conditions under which political liberty may be set aside for economic advantage. He does not, in other words, present the second principle as grounds for overriding the first. Rather, he presents the second principle as stating the grounds on which the presumption (of equal distribution) can be set aside. What is at stake, quite clearly, is the question when unequal distribution of payoffs may justly be substituted for equal distribution of payoffs, *not* the quite different question when a certain pattern of payoffs of one sort of good (wealth, etc.) may be invoked as justification for deviating from an equal distribution of a different sort of good (namely, liberty). This interpretation is reinforced by the fact that the very notion of "equal liberty" in a *distributive* sense is thoroughly unclear. To say of two persons that they are "equal before the law" is to say something quite precise about the way they are treated in law. To say that all persons shall be equal before the law is, in the context of late eighteenth- and early nineteenth-century political theory, to say something important and significant about the legal and political arrangements of a society. But to say that all persons shall receive "the most extensive liberty compatible with a like liberty for all" is, to put it mildly, mysterious. Unless we invoke some quite metaphorical notion of a "moral space of individual rights" and make some pseudo-formal passes of a quasi-topological sort at the notion of compact spheres of individual rights expanding and being deformed continuously until they have filled the entire social space, or whatever, the no-

39

tion of the "most extensive (political) liberty compatible with a like liberty for all" simply cannot be made clear. But we can make very clear indeed the notion of a most extensive equal distribution of goods.

The second consideration supporting my interpretation of the first principle is the fact that it makes Rawls's "theorem" seem at least initially plausible. The proof of the theorem will simply involve an invocation of the conception of Pareto optimality, with the understanding that the quasi-ordering of alternative distributions is to be made with respect to the original, or baseline situation of equal distribution. Such a line of reasoning in support of the two principles will make sense only if the first principle is construed as a prima facie rule of equal distribution and the second principle is construed as an excuse for deviations from distributive equality.

With regard to Principle IIa, it suffices to point out that Rawls here invokes what is sometimes called strong Pareto preference, rather than weak Pareto preference. Inequalities are to be justified not merely on the grounds that they make no one worse off and at least one person better off. Rather, they are to be justified only if they make *everyone* better off. This is a strong requirement, and it is not clear whether Rawls really means to insist on it. Suppose, to resurrect our example of the shoe shop, that the shift to the new system increases the net income of the shop just exactly to $650,000 a year, so that, after the fifty unaffected workers receive $10,000 each and the ten fast workers receive their $15,000 each, there is no inequality surplus left to sweeten the deal. The fifty regular workers are indifferent between the two practices, since their duties and rewards are the same in each. By hypothesis, the ten fast workers prefer the new arrangement, under which they work harder and earn more. It would seem to be collectively rational for the players in the bargaining game to rank the unequal arrangement ahead of the baseline of perfect equality. After all, what save sheer envy at the improvement experienced by the ten could motivate the fifty to vote against such a ranking? And since each player will recognize that there might be situations in which he is one of the beneficiaries of the inequality, he will wish to establish such a ranking as a general principle.[12]

Eventually, Rawls shifted to an interpretation of Principle IIa according to which the condition of the least advantaged is to be maximized (and then each higher position's condition maximized in lexicographic order). This change had the incidental effect of mooting the choice between weak and strong Pareto preference.

Principle IIb is also susceptible of varying interpretations. "Open to all" may mean, among other things, open to all in a fair competition, or open to all in some sort of rotation, or open to all by a random assignment. Relatively soon after the appearance of "Justice as Fairness," Rawls had opted for the notion of fair competition, but, as we shall soon see, certain problems remain with Principle IIb.

---

[12] Welfare economics treats problems of distribution completely independently of the constraints imposed by techniques of production. By making some powerful continuity assumptions, it is then easily shown that strong and weak Pareto preference are equivalent. Whenever a single individual prefers situation A to situation B, because B gives him more of whatever is being handed out, we can simply take some of the extra away from him, divide it up as many times as necessary, and spread it around so that everyone gets at least a little bit more. But if $15,000 is the lowest wage for which workers will do the faster paced work, then lowering that wage even a little will force the shop back into the original conditions of production. This is a small point, but it has wide ramifications, some of which are explored more fully in the concluding section of this essay.

THE APPLICATION OF THE PRINCIPLES

Do Principles I and II provide us with a clear and unambiguous standard by which to evaluate actual or proposed practices? The question, needless to say, is *not* whether they provide us with a correct standard of *just* practices. The correctness of the standard is supposed to be established, in some way or other, by the fact that the two principles are the solution of the bargaining game Rawls has defined. But before we can even consider the plausibility of such a claim, we must ask whether the principles do in fact provide us with a ranking of practices.

Suppose that a society has adopted the two principles; how would they be applied when a dispute arose? There are three sorts of claims that might be brought by a member of the society against one of its practices, corresponding to the conditions laid down in Principle I, Principle IIa, and Principle IIb. I take it that the invocation of Principle I poses no problems (assuming, as I shall, that it is an equal distribution principle and not a quasi-political equal liberty principle). Principle IIb poses some rather tricky problems that we will defer for the moment. Consider, then, Principle IIa, which is the heart of Rawls's conception of justice.

What does it mean to say that inequalities do or do not work out for everyone's advantage? Presumably, it can only mean that everyone can reasonably expect to be better off *with* the inequality than without. But better off than what? Rawls says, better off than under the same practice without the inequality. In short, the practice with the inequality is unanimously preferred to the practice without the inequality. But this raises as many questions as it answers. Suppose that the practice under review is a factory in which some workers are foremen and others tend machines, and in which the foremen both

42

earn more money and work less hard (because the labor of direction is less taxing than the labor of machine-tending). What would be *the same practice without the inequalities*? One could equalize the pay, of course, but one could not eliminate the differential burdens of the various roles without altering the division of labor itself, thereby altering the practice.

The problem is compounded when we are called upon to compare two practices that serve the same purpose but that define different numbers of roles and distribute individuals to them in different numbers. How, for example, shall we compare one mode of factory production in which a rather highly stratified system of roles defines ten separate positions, each with its characteristic functions and payoffs, with a second mode of production (designed to produce the same commodity) in which a simpler, more integrated grouping of functions results in three positions, unequally paid and functionally differentiated? When we are asked whether each representative man can reasonably expect to be advantaged by the second practice relative to the first, which roles are we to compare with which? As we move, in imagination, from practice to practice, what device enables us to pick out in each possible practice the *same* representative man, so that we are able to ask whether in any of the imagined practices he can reasonably expect to be better off than in some actual practice under scrutiny?

Once we recall that Rawls is employing the notion of Pareto preference, it should be obvious that it poses for him all the problems that are so familiar in welfare economics. "Unanimously preferred to," in both its weak and strong senses, only defines a quasi-ordering. Two practices, P' and P^*, may both be unanimously preferred to a third practice, P, although neither P' nor P^* is unanimously preferred to the other. For example, capitalism might be unanimously preferred to what Engels called primitive communism (assuming that one could identify the appropriate "representative men" under capitalism and assuming, too, what recent anthropological works deny, that the typical primitive man is worse off than the worst off representative man under capitalism); and feudalism might also be unanimously preferred to primitive communism (leaving to one side violations of Principle IIb); and yet capitalism might *not* be unanimously preferred to feudalism, because it might be, as Marx thought (but recent research tends to deny), that peasants who moved off the feudal manors into the towns and cities suffered an absolute decline in their level of well-being. If we were to employ Rawls's principles, we would be forced to conclude that capitalism was just relative to primitive communism and unjust relative to feudalism, which is, to say the least, an odd way to employ the notion of social justice. The source of the problem, grammatically speaking, is that the phrase "to everyone's advantage" sounds like a positive but is actually a comparative (i.e., it sounds like "good" but functions like "better").

An analogous problem arises when someone comes forward to propose an alteration in an existing practice. So long as there is an inequality surplus, there will exist some way to distribute it so that every representative position under the new practice is better off than the corresponding position under the existing practice (assuming, once again, that we can solve the vexing problem of matching up corresponding roles in different practices). Hence, the proposed practice will be unanimously preferred to the existing practice (and hence *more just!* again, an odd usage). But there will in general be many different ways of carrying out such a distribution, each of which is unanimously preferred to the

44

original practice and no one of which can possibly be unanimously preferred to any other (since, for a fixed inequality surplus, every alteration in the distribution of it will involve taking a bit of the surplus from one representative man to give more to another).

Consider for a moment the simplest sort of case that could fall under Rawls's Principle IIa. Assume a practice, P, which defines m roles, such that the number of persons occupying the ith role is n_i, and the reward or payoff (assumed, for convenience, to be money) to the ith role is P_i. It follows that the net income or bundle of wealth being divided among the participants in the practice is given by the expression:

$$\text{Payoff to } P = \sum_{i=1}^{m} n_i P_i.$$

Let us assume that all of the P_i are the same except for a single payoff, P_j, which is larger, and that the total output of the practice with this inequality is larger than without it. There are two possibilities. The first possibility is that there is no inequality surplus. The individuals drawn to the jth role by the promise of the larger payoff P_j increase the total output or productivity of the practice enough, but only enough, to cover the cost of the higher payoff required to get them into role j. In other words, if P_j were reduced even slightly, so as to make some surplus available for redistribution, role j would cease to be attractive enough to draw into it those individuals whose special skills or harder work result in the increased output. In this case, although Rawls would not judge practice P to be just (because the inequality works out only to the advantage of the jth representative man, not to everyone's advantage), we might extend his principles and call P just. If there is an inequality surplus, however—if, that is to say, the output of the practice with the increased payoff to the jth position is more than enough to cover the minimal increase to the jth position necessary to draw into that role people whose work will result in the larger output—then there will be many non-Pareto-comparable ways of distributing that surplus. Each one of them will be "just," on Rawls's principles, relative to the practice without the inequality in payoffs; and each one of them will be *unjust* relative to each other one. Once we complicate the situation even slightly, for example, by considering cases in which the increased output of the practice requires extra payoffs to two or more roles, then things become utterly unmanageable. And this still assumes that we are comparing practices that are identical save for payoffs.

(It is worth noting here that Rawls's initial conception of the two principles is strictly along *micro*-economic lines. We are presumably to assume that the changes in payoffs to the several roles of the practice will have no significant effect on the economy as a whole.) Hence we can speak easily of money redistributions within the practice without worrying either about inflation or about shifts in relative prices. If the difference principle were to be invoked not for a ranking of small-scale practices but for an evaluation of the broad, basic economic institutions of the entire society (as Rawls tells us, in later versions of the model, that it *is* to be employed), then we should have to ask very complicated questions, such as whether a major redistribution in income will alter relative prices in such a way as either to negate the supposed redistributive effect or else to make the states of affairs before and after the redistribution not plausibly comparable. These so-called indexing problems, which arise when we attempt to estimate the relative welfare of individuals at two different stages of a society's history or in two quite different economies, will be especially vexing

46

to Rawls, once he starts to apply his principles to macro-economic institutional arrangements.

ARE THE TWO PRINCIPLES THE SOLUTION OF THE BARGAINING GAME?

Finally, we must ask whether the players in Rawls's bargaining game would choose the two principles he has proposed, assuming that they can make coherent sense of them and figure out (as we have been unable to) how they would be used to rank alternative practices and alternative distributions to a given practice. The answer is quite simply no, and the reasons why they would not be chosen go a long way toward explaining Rawls's invention of the veil of ignorance.

Let us begin by focusing our attention on Principle IIb. As I have noted, "open to all" can be interpreted in at least several different plausible ways, including "assigned on the basis of fair competition with regard to the skills or qualities needed to do the job well," and "assigned on the basis of a lottery." In the former case, we may suppose that the most competent individuals would tend to occupy the positions offering special rewards (the rationale, roughly speaking, of social stratification in modern functionalist sociology), whereas in the latter case the positions would be filled by lot, with the most desirable positions going to those who happened to win the lottery.

What would happen if these two variants of Principle IIb were proposed for adoption (assuming that the players in the game had provisionally agreed to Principles I and IIa)? On first thought, we might assume that everyone would opt for assignment by competition. Obviously, a society run on that principle would achieve maximum efficiency, hence have the largest total wealth to distribute, and so hold out the possibility of practices

47

unanimously preferable to any achieved under some other set of ground rules. But let us consider the matter more closely (as we may be sure the members of this society would do, since they are rationally self-interested).

Rawls has stipulated that the individuals be "sufficiently equal in power and ability to guarantee that in normal circumstances none is able to dominate the other." This still leaves a fair degree of variation in native talent and ambition sufficient at any rate to give some individuals an edge over others in an open competition for favored positions. It would be reasonably well known to each individual what his talents and abilities were relative to the other players. Some would be aware that they stood rather high in ability, others that they were relatively disadvantaged. Now these latter would say to themselves, "It is true that the total wealth of the society will be greater if positions are filled by competition; and if I really had an equal chance of getting the top jobs, it would make sense for me to agree to the competitive version of Principle IIb. But I am not as likely to get one of those jobs as are my more talented fellow citizens; in fact, since I am among the least talented members of this society, the odds of my ending up at the bottom of the heap in a fair competition are pretty high. If positions were distributed by lot, on the other hand, I would have a better chance at those top jobs, even though they might pay less because of the decreased efficiency of a system that puts the likes of me in positions of authority and importance. Taking all in all (or, technically, estimating the expected value of the two gambles), it is in my rational self-interest to hold out for the random assignment interpretation of Principle IIb."[13]

[13] Notice, by the way, that this line of reasoning in no way violates the non-envy assumption. The less talented do not begrudge the more talented the higher pay they will earn under a system open to

The more able members of the society would perform an analogous calculation and come to the directly opposed conclusion that *their* self-interest was best served by the competitive version of Principle IIb. There is no single set of rules to which everyone in the society could commit himself in the firm and rational expectation that he had done the best for himself that he could reasonably hope.

It would appear, therefore, that the bargaining would simply grind to a halt. But there are ways out of the impasse. Since each individual desires to reach some agreement, and since the two principles, under either version of IIb, are unanimously preferable to having no way of settling disputes at all, it would be irrational for either side to allow the bargaining to break down. No rational argument can persuade the less talented that they ought, in their own interest, to adopt competition; and no rational argument can persuade the more talented that they ought, in their own interest, to accept random assignment. The proper game-theoretic solution is therefore to randomize: a toss of a coin can settle the issue. This *would* be to everyone's advantage, since if each interpretation is unanimously preferable to no agreement, then the average of the two will be also. Of course, any weighted average of the two of the form $[p\text{IIb} + (1 - p)\text{IIb}']$ will also be unanimously preferable to no agreement, so perhaps we ought not to assume too readily that the bargaining game will issue in a unanimously agreed upon set of principles.

Analogous problems arise with regard to the adoption of Principle IIa. Rawls asserts that in their deliberations, the players will be guided by what is called the maximin

talents. The less talented, who turn out to have a quite adequate grasp of the principles of prudential reason, simply make a non-envious self-interested calculation.

principle of decision under uncertainty.[14] "These principles express the conditions in accordance with which each is the least unwilling [this is the maximin principle] to have his interests limited in the design of the practices, given the competing interests of the others, on the supposition that the interests of others will be limited likewise" (138–39). As Rawls rather colorfully puts it, the restrictions "might be thought of as those a person would keep in mind if he were designing a practice in which his enemy were to assign him his place" (139).

But why should the players choose the extremely conservative maximin principle as their guide in their deliberations? The conceit of protecting oneself against one's enemy, taken literally, is inappropriate, inasmuch as the players are not envious and hence, construing that assumption in a suitably general sense of the term "envy," do not have any interest in bringing their opponents low. The least talented might at first hold out for Principle IIa, on the grounds that, since they were the most probable candidates for the lowest positions, they were unwilling to take a chance that the lowest positions would actually be worse paid than under conditions of absolute equality of distribution. The more talented, of course, would prefer some form of average utility principle, since they could reasonably expect (especially if the competitive version of IIb had been agreed to) that their payoffs would be pulling the average up rather than dragging it down. In this situation, with each player making the best estimates possible of the reasonably expectable consequences of the application of different principles, all manner of proposals and counterproposals

[14] That is, the rule that tells us to *max*imize the *min*imum payoff available to us. See Part Four below, and any game theory text, such as R. D. Luce and H. Raiffa, *Games and Decisions* (John Wiley & Sons, 1957).

can be imagined, no one of which would seem to have a solid chance of winning unanimity in all plays of such a bargaining game. For example, the less advantaged might agree to an average utility form of IIa, which would permit production-increasing inequalities achieved at the price of an absolute lowering of the least well paid representative man, in return for a lottery-version of Principle IIb, which would level up their risks of ending in the least advantaged roles.

In his "sketch of a proof," it seems to me, Rawls slips into a fairly simple logical error. There is no question that the players in the bargaining game would all willingly move from a practice offering a given set of payoffs to a new version of the practice that raised the expectations of every representative man. Non-envy and positive marginal utility for money guarantee that. So we may assume that they will endorse the principle "*Always* choose a unanimously preferred practice or distribution in a practice to a given practice or distribution when one is offered." But it does not at all follow that they will endorse the much more controversial principle "*Only* choose one practice or distribution over another when the first is unanimously preferred to the second."

There is no need to belabor the inadequacies of the first form of Rawls's model, especially since he himself soon abandoned it for many of the reasons we have been exploring. The two principal sources of difficulty are, first, the inability of the relation of Pareto-preferability to provide an adequate ordering of alternative practices, or of alternative patterns of distribution within a practice; and second, the impossibility of achieving unanimity among a group of players who, in a manner of speaking, know too much about themselves and their fellow-players.

Technically, Rawls's game is an *n-person non-zero-sum cooperative game*. It is *n*-person because any finite number of persons may play; it is non-zero-sum because the preferences of the players are not strictly competitive (all of the players, for example, prefer any one of a number of possible outcomes to the baseline or degenerate outcome of no agreement at all); and it is a cooperative game in the sense that "players have complete freedom of preplay communication to make joint *binding* agreements." (Luce and Raiffa, p. 89; italics in the original.)

Rawls does not tell us how the game is actually played, but we may suppose that the rules are these: the players are arranged arbitrarily in some order (alphabetically, for example); the first player makes a move, which consists of announcing, in a voice that can be heard clearly by all, a principle or set of principles for evaluating the practices in which the players, as members of society, are or may become engaged. The second player then makes a move, which consists of announcing a principle or set of principles. The players make moves of this sort, proceeding through the list of players again and again until the referee announces that *n* players in succession have made identically the same proposal (not necessarily beginning with player 1, of course). At that point, the referee declares the game terminated, and the proposal which has been made *n* times in a row becomes the set of principles which, henceforth, the players are committed to abide by in the evaluation of their social practices and institutions.

[15] Here, as elsewhere, I rely heavily on R. D. Luce and H. Raiffa, *Games and Decisions*, and T. Schelling, *The Strategy of Conflict* (Harvard University Press, 1960).

Now the first thing to notice is that since there is no time limit on the game, and nothing at all has been said about non-rule-governed time constraints (boredom, a need to get the crops planted, etc.), there is no reason for any rational player to offer a compromise principle. Since moves are cost-free, the only rational thing for each player to do is to propose, "Let everything be done exactly as I desire from this day forward." There is a non-zero probability that all the other $n - 1$ players will stupidly agree, in which case he will well and truly have won the game!

If a time limit is imposed, however, the symmetry of the game is destroyed, for the last person to make a move before the time is up is in a different position from the next to the last, and so forth. As Thomas Schelling has pointed out, once we give up the assumption of symmetry, it becomes vitally important exactly where in the order of players you are, in relation to the deadline. In Rawls's game, suppose that each move (each announcement of a proposed set of principles) takes a certain minimum finite time = t *seconds*. The player who gets to move exactly nt *seconds* before the termination time has an enormous advantage over all the others. He can propose a set of principles which, although they can reasonably be expected to benefit him unduly, still are such that it would be in each player's interest to accept them rather than to fall back into the "state of nature" condition of having no rules agreed upon at all. The remaining players are now stuck. If anyone of them fails, on this last go-round, to enunciate the principles of the favored player, there will not be enough time to arrive at any other set of principles, and so they will fall back into a state of nature. Being rational and non-envious, they will agree to the biased proposal, much as they will regret the fact that the favored player had so great a bargaining advantage over them. (See Schelling, Appendix B, especially pp. 274–75, note 11.)

The difficulties just outlined could be overcome by changing the game into a non-cooperative game, in which "absolutely no preplay communication is permitted between the players." (Luce and Raiffa, p. 89.) The game would then become what is called a coordination game: each player would write his proposed principles on a slip of paper and hand it to the referee; if all the slips of paper contained identically the same principles, they would become the rules of the society; otherwise, the society would lapse back into the state of nature. Schelling has explored such coordination games with great imagination and industry, and he demonstrates quite persuasively (in my judgment) that successful coordination depends upon the influence of factors that are extraneous to the purely formal model of the game, and in the game theoretic sense irrational. (Such as the existence of cultural traditions which all the participants know about and know the other participants know about, or even the presence of a prominently displayed sign in the bargaining room with the motto "share and share alike" on it.) In the first form of the game, in which the players know who they are and what positions they occupy in society, there is no ground at all for supposing that a coordination game will result in a unanimously chosen set of principles, and even less reason, if that be possible, for supposing that one and only one set of principles will be the outcome of every play of the game. In the final form of the model, after the "veil of ignorance" has been lowered (more of this later), the choice situation has so thoroughly changed that totally different considerations must be appealed to by Rawls in defense of his claim that his two principles of justice are the solution to the game.

Finally, a word about the maximin rule of choice might be helpful here, even though the subject will be gone into at length in Part Four. In two-person zero-sum games, it turns out that there are very impressive (though by no means incontrovertible) arguments in favor of calculating the worst that might happen to you as a result of each strategy, or line of play available, and then choosing the strategy which has the "best worst." Maximizing your minimum payoff, or maximin, has a variety of mathematical properties in two-person zero-sum games that recommend it as a rational procedure. Since two-person zero-sum games do indeed have the characteristic that whatever you gain your opponent loses, and vice versa, there is a certain literary appropriateness in playing as though your worst enemy were going to determine, within the limits of his power, what happened to you. But in n-person non-zero-sum games no meaning can be given to the notion that one player gains what the other player loses. (Note: because of the way in which utility functions are defined, it is not, for example, possible to distinguish between non-zero-sum games in which "everyone can win" and non-zero-sum games in which "everyone can lose." The feature known as "zero-summedness" is merely a consequence of the strictly competitive character of the players' preferences and the permissibility of linear transformations of the utility functions.)

Consequently, it is not at all obvious, either mathematically or philosophically, that maximin is the rational choice rule. There are perfectly good arguments for choosing so as to maximize average utility, and if that strikes a player as a trifle risky, he can always weight his averages in order to express his degree of aversion to risk (over and above the weight he has already given to various payoff bundles in the construction of his utility function). Neither in the cooperative nor in the non-cooperative version of Rawls's game is there any reason to suppose that rational players will always agree to, or coordinate on, the two "principles of justice."

VI

The Second Form of the Model

AT this point, Rawls makes two major alterations in his theory, clearly for the express purpose of meeting the sorts of objections we have explored in our examination of the first form of the model. The two changes are first the problem-laden device of the veil of ignorance, and second the substitution of the difference principle in its "least advantaged representative man" form for the simple principle of Pareto preferability.

Before examining these two theoretical innovations, it might be worth pausing for a moment to take note of a rather odd characteristic of Rawls's exposition. Very early on, by 1958 or before, Rawls had settled upon a formula for expressing his "two principles of justice." Despite certain unclarities, which we have already examined, the principles as stated had a fairly natural interpretation to any ordinary reader of English. Roughly speaking, they dictated that a society should choose as its baseline the equal distribution point closest to its production frontier, and should then deviate from that point only in order to move to some other point, Pareto-preferred to the baseline point, at which the relatively favored positions were open to all in fair competition. These principles, Rawls claimed, were at one and the same time an accurate reconstruction of our settled moral convictions about matters of institutional justice (more of this later) and the solution to a bargaining game so defined as to capture the essential notion of a society of rationally self-interested individuals ready to commit themselves to a set of principles.

When the unclarities, inadequacies, and inconsistencies of these two claims about his principles become apparent to Rawls, his obvious move is to give up his formula, and search instead for a different set of principles that meet the theoretical demands he wishes to place upon them. In short, if the first proposed solution to a bargaining game turns out to be wrong, look for a second. But Rawls takes a quite different tack altogether. He treats the original formulation of the two principles as given, *ex cathedra* as it were, and then hunts about for some way of "interpreting" the words that will make defensible sense. (Thus, in "Distributive Justice,"[16] even though he has substantially altered his theory, he restates the principles in language that is, save for the substitution of "institutions" for "practices" and a few grammatical emendations, word-for-word identical with that of the "Justice as Fairness" formulation. He now says, as though he were seeking to decipher a puzzling text, that "it is not clear what is meant by saying that inequalities must be to the advantage of every representative man" (62). He first suggests comparing the institution under examination with some "historically relevant benchmark" (63). Then he proposes straight Pareto-optimality as the "meaning." Finally he hits upon "a third interpretation" (66), namely the maximization of the expectations of the least-advantaged representative man. Similar "interpretations," later on, lead Rawls to the principle of the priority of liberty and to other theoretical changes in the original model.

Now, it is perfectly sensible to treat a set of words in this manner if they come to us with some stamp of authority—if, for example, they are the words of God.

[16] Laslett and Runciman, *Philosophy, Politics, and Society* (Barnes & Noble, Inc., 1967), third series, pp. 58–82. Parenthetical references in this section are to this essay.

When reason conflicts with the apparent meaning of God's commands, one natural (although not the only) response is to interpret the command. One cannot simply change it, since it is God's word, but one can cast about for a meaning conformable to reason and moral intuition. The same sort of procedure makes some sense when one is dealing with the writings of a great but obscure thinker. Some philosophers on occasion have deep insights that are rich in suggestion and promise, but whose expression is obscure or confused. We gamble our time and energy, in a manner of speaking, when we seek an interpretation of their words that will cohere with their basic theoretical orientation and yet also make defensible philosophical sense. But there is something slightly odd about a philosopher treating his own words in this manner. Surely, we want to say, Rawls should either decide that his original solution to the bargaining game was correct, and defend it, or else decide that it was wrong, and change it. But why decide that it was wrong, and then split the difference by sticking with the words and changing their meaning?

Eventually, though with what I can only construe as great reluctance, Rawls revises the actual wording of his two principles. But this deeply conservative style of intellectual development is revealing and important as a clue to the structure of Rawls's thought. It is highly instructive to compare Rawls with another moral and social philosopher in the Anglo-American tradition, John Stuart Mill. Throughout his long life, Mill struggled to free himself from the narrow conceptual confines of the simple utilitarian faith in which his father, James Mill, and his godfather, Jeremy Bentham, raised him. In books such as his *Principles of Political Economy*, we can see Mill considering, taking account of, acknowledging the merits of, the most varied competing schools of thought, from romanticism and idealism to utopian socialism. There is almost no criticism one can bring against Mill that he has not somewhere discussed and even conceded. Yet despite it all, he remains, fundamentally, an unreconstructed utilitarian.

Rawls seems to me to exhibit very much this same set of mind. Early in the development of his philosophy, he hit upon the device of the bargaining game and the two principles as its solution. He clung to it through all the revisions, complications, and adjustments of the theory, and it dominates the exposition of *A Theory of Justice*, notwithstanding the extremely modest and concessive tone of the concluding chapter. Later in this essay, I shall suggest a number of reasons for doubting that the two principles, in any of their forms, would be chosen by individuals in any of the various original positions sketched by Rawls. But I think it fair to say that Rawls has thought of, and thought through, most of the objections I and other critics advance, even though he sometimes neither answers the objections nor alters his theory to meet them.

THE VEIL OF IGNORANCE

The veil of ignorance first appears in "Distributive Justice." In describing the situation of the players in the bargaining game, Rawls says that they are to be conceived as located

in a suitably defined initial situation one of the significant features of which is that no one knows his position in society, nor even his place in the distribution of natural talents and abilities. The principles of justice to which all are forever bound are chosen in the absence of this sort of specific information. A veil of ignorance prevents anyone from being advantaged or disadvantaged by the contingencies of social class and fortune; and hence the bargaining problems which arise in everyday life from the possession of this knowledge do not affect the choice of principles. [60]

Needless to say, the veil of ignorance is an analytical device, not a utopian proposal nor an account of a primeval naiveté. The effect of the device is to stipulate that, in their reasoning, the players of the bargaining game are to abstract from, and hence not to take into account, the particularities of their fortune or natural and social endowments. The constraint is analogous to the requirement in pure geometry that one abstract from the particular characteristics of the figure under consideration when proving a theorem and attend only to certain of its mathematical properties. Indeed, since Rawls thinks that the reasoning of the players is not deductive but, in some sense, constructive, one might say that he imposes on his players the same sort of constraint that Kant thought was imposed on us by the form of pure intuition in our pure mathematical reasoning.

The veil of ignorance has many attractions, from Rawls's point of view. First, and most obviously, it dissolves some of the strongest objections to the first form of the model. As we saw, the two principal reasons why rational players could not be expected to choose Rawls's two principles were, first, that their knowledge of their own special talents and abilities would lead them to disagree over a principle for assigning individuals to unequally rewarded positions and, second, that this very same knowledge would lead the more able to favor principles that permitted slight reductions in the payoffs to the least favored in return for substantial increases to all the other positions. The impossibility of reaching agreement, I suggested, would result not in unanimous agreement to Rawls's two principles, as the only way to avoid a breakdown of bargaining, but rather in any one of a number of mixed or randomly selected weighted combinations of principles favoring different sectors of the society of players. But the veil of ignorance denies to players precisely the information that would lead them into these sorts of disagreements. Hence it offers some hope of transforming the bargaining game into one having, in the requisite technical sense, a *solution*.

The veil of ignorance has positive attractions as well, and these obviously weigh very heavily with Rawls. In the first place, by denying to the players any information of their "place in the distribution of natural talents and abilities," it inclines them toward adoption of a principle that will treat those talents and abilities as social, rather than personal, resources. Not knowing where he ranks in the distribution, each player will, Rawls thinks, seek a principle that makes the fruit of those talents and abilities available to the members of society generally. The net result will be to eliminate what Rawls and many other moral philosophers consider the social injustice of rewarding individuals for the accident of their possession of economically profitable native talents.

The veil of ignorance also has the effect of forcing players to adopt a generalized point of view that bears a strong resemblance to what some moral philosophers call "the moral point of view."[17] The facts that are denied to the players by the veil are just those facts that it seems inappropriate to take into account when making moral, as opposed to merely prudential, judgments. If Rawls can show that a group of prudentially rational agents, each seeking his own rational self-interest, would by ig-

[17] In Part Three of this essay, I shall discuss at length the so-called Kantian interpretation of the original position and its relationship to the veil of ignorance.

noring the particularities of their individual conditions arrive at precisely the set of principles that would be endorsed from a moral point of view, then he will have made a significant theoretical advance. In effect, he will have shown that moral conclusions can be reached, without abandoning the prudential standpoint and positing a moral outlook, merely by pursuing one's prudential reasoning under certain procedural bargaining and knowledge constraints. The maneuver thus promises to circumvent the endless, indecisive arguing and counterarguing of the various competing schools of moral theory. Since Rawls must have appreciated the power of the idea, and since at first it seemed to solve the problems of the first form of the model, it is not difficult to understand why he adopted the veil of ignorance as a modification of his theory.

THE DIFFERENCE PRINCIPLE

The second major change was the rewriting of Principle IIa in the form of what has come to be called the "difference principle." Rawls introduces it, somewhat disingenuously, as the third possible "interpretation" of the language of the original two principles:

> There is, however, a third interpretation which is immediately suggested by the previous remarks [concerning the inadequacies of Pareto-optimality as a principle], and this is to choose some social position by reference to which the pattern of expectations as a whole is to be judged, and then to maximize with respect to the expectations of this representative man consistent with the demands of equal liberty and equality of opportunity. Now, the one obvious candidate is the representative man of those who are least favored by the system of institutional inequalities. [66]

63

The shift to the "least advantaged" version of the difference principle immediately solves two of the most serious problems posed by the first form of the model. First of all, it makes possible a complete ordering, and not merely a quasi-ordering, of alternative practices, institutions, sets of institutions, societies, or whatever. As between two institutions, one merely identifies the least advantaged representative man under each and compares the payoffs assigned to "him" (not, of course, necessarily the same individual or group of individuals in each case). The institution that assigns a greater payoff to the least advantaged man is to be favored, no matter what the total output, or total welfare, or pattern of other payoffs may be. Since for any two institutions, the least advantaged representative man in the first will either be better off, as well off, or worse off, than the least advantaged man in the second, and since this sense of "better off than" is transitive, the new version of the difference principle will define a complete weak ordering.[18]

The second virtue of the new difference principle is that it dissolves the puzzle of comparing practices with different numbers of roles, defined in ways that do not permit natural or easy comparison. Each practice will have to define a least-advantaged role, even if it is a practice with only one role. To be sure, this change will permit us to make some rather odd comparisons, such as, say, a comparison between monogamous marriage and the Volvo plant system of automobile assembly. Theoret-

[18] Once again, it is necessary to add the qualification that no account is being taken of shifts in relative prices or changes in the identity and nature of commodities. Since we are comparing the payoffs to "representative men" in different practices, and since the identity of the least advantaged representative man may change from practice to practice, Rawls must shift from considerations of utility to considerations of intersubjectively comparable payoffs, whether of money or of bundles of commodities.

ically, there is nothing in Rawls's principle to prevent us from asking which practice is to be preferred and then answering it by comparing the least advantaged representative man in the Volvo system with the least advantaged representative man (probably the woman) in the practice of monogamous marriage. If we feel uncomfortable at having to choose between the family car and the family, we can always define some third practice, combining the two, in which the least advantaged representative man is better off than under either of the other two alone.

VII

A Critique of the Second Form of the Model

THE veil of ignorance and the new form of the difference principle mark a major advance over the first form of the model, but upon inspection we immediately realize, as Rawls must have done, that further changes and elaborations are necessary before this new model can serve the purposes Rawls intends.

The first difficulty, of course, is that, unless we specify exactly how much the veil of ignorance obscures and how much it leaves available to the occupants of the original position, we shall be unable to deduce anything at all about their reasoning processes. So something will have to be said about the sorts of general knowledge or particular information that the players retain after they have entered the bargaining game and have forgotten who in particular they are.

A second problem, potentially more serious than this first, is posed by the veil of ignorance. In the original model, the players were assumed to be rationally self-interested individuals with fully developed, self-consciously defined aims, interests, purposes, and plans. But following the lead of classical utilitarianism and modern welfare economics, Rawls made no substantive assumptions about the character of those purposes or interests. It was not assumed, for example, that they valued the delights of the mind over the pleasures of the body, or that they either cherished or despised the company of their fellow creatures. The only constraint assumed to operate on their preferences was the familiar assumption of positive marginal utility for whatever goods were being distributed by the practice in question.[19]

Under the veil of ignorance, however, the players have no idea whatsoever of their purposes, plans, and interests. It would appear, therefore, that they can say nothing at all about how they would like their institutions to be arranged. To be sure, they can each assert some general and vacuous claim, such as that when they find out what it is that they want, they wish the practice of which they are a part to assign to their role in it some set of rewards that helps them to get whatever they want. But in the bargaining that is to determine the choice of the constructive principles for the evaluation of social practices, it is hard to see how the players will reason so long as they are totally ignorant of every substantive fact of their desires and purposes. So something will also have to be said about the sorts of purposes that the players have in their real existence, though nothing of course may be said that differentiates them from one another or that enables them to infer in any way their actual talents, abilities, or interests.

The difference principle also poses some new problems, even while it is solving old ones. The first problem concerns the scope of the principle, the sorts of cases to which it is to be thought to apply. In the original model of his theory, Rawls talked a good bit about roles and games, in a way that suggested a rather small-scale notion of the justice of practices. We were encouraged to think of the game of baseball, or the organization of a fac-

[19] With the further anti-trivializing condition that the term "goods" was to be understood objectively and socially, rather than subjectively and individually. For the contrary view, see I. M. D. Little, *A Critique of Welfare Economics* (2nd ed., Oxford at Clarendon Press, 1957), p. 16.

tory, or the hierarchical authority structure of an army. As I have several times observed, Rawls seemed to assume implicitly that his principle would be applied to practices each one of which was sufficiently small-scale, in relation to the society of which it was a part, that changes in its pattern of rewards would have negligible effects on the total economy of the society. So long as the players could be thought of as identifiable individuals bargaining in full possession of the details of their situation, this construal of Rawls's model made sense. But once we move to the veil of ignorance version, in which the players are conceived as adopting an impersonal, perhaps even a timeless, perspective, the small-scale or micro-interpretation of the two principles appears inappropriate. It is more plausible to construe the bargaining game as determining, for all time, the most fundamental structure of the economy and society. In the next form of the model, accordingly, Rawls explicitly restricts the difference principle to macro-economic and macro-social arrangements. This in turn, as we shall see, generates some exceedingly knotty problems.

A second difficulty, which has been much noted and commented upon by recent critics of Rawls, concerns some of the counterintuitive implications of the revised difference principle. In the original Pareto-preference form, the principle defined a quasi-ordering that, so far as it went, was quite attractive as a rule of collective choice. Since inequalities were required to work out to everyone's advantage, a practice judged just by Principle IIa could be certain to win unanimous approval. The new principle, to be sure, establishes a complete rather than merely a quasi-ordering, but in so doing it commits the players to seriously questionable judgments of relative preferability. Since this point has been made by many critics of Rawls and (characteristically) is recognized by Rawls himself, a single example will suffice to indicate the nature of the problem.[20]

Imagine a social system of economic institutions and practices, in which a number of functionally differentiated productive roles are differentially rewarded, but in which the gap between the best and worst rewarded jobs is not very large. Let us imagine (if indeed this would be true) that the narrowness of the gap between different levels of reward has the consequence that there is not a very efficient sorting of talents. Since the payoff of the more highly skilled jobs is not much greater than that for unskilled jobs, individuals are not strongly motivated to submit themselves to the additional training necessary to acquire the requisite skills. What is more, certain sorts of very highly skilled jobs do not even exist in the system because no one is prepared to make the enormous personal commitment necessary to prepare for them. Now suppose that a revision of this system of production and distribution is proposed, involving a more highly differentiated work structure, with a society-wide upgrading of job skills, and requiring for its efficient operation a much greater spread in the reward structure. In this revised system, every representative man *save the least well-off* is considerably better off than before (assuming that a plausible cross-system comparison can be made in view of the change in the number of roles), but the least well-off representative man is slightly worse off. Finally, and most important, let us assume that there is *no* inequality surplus out of which transfers could be paid to the least advantaged

[20] See, for example, the opening sections of John C. Harsanyi's essay, "Can the Maximin Principle Serve as a Basis for Morality? A Critique of John Rawls' Theory," *APSR*, Vol. 69, No. 2 (June 1975), pp. 594–606. See also the very sophisticated discussion by Douglas Rae, "Maximin Justice and an Alternative Principle of General Advantage," ibid., pp. 630–47.

class. The system calls for so sensitive a matching of talents to jobs that if anything significant in the way of rewards were taken from the better-off jobs to compensate the least advantaged, the efficiency of the system would be reduced to a point at which the society would be worse off than before. According to Rawls, rational persons in the original position would adopt a principle (the difference principle) that would rule out moving to this revised system from the original system, no matter how great the gains to every class but the least advantaged, no matter how marginal the disadvantage to the least advantaged, and no matter how small the size of that least advantaged class![21] Rawls will need some very powerful and plausible rule of rational choice to justify a selection of principles along such lines in the original position. His proposal, as we shall see shortly, is the so-called maximin rule of choice under uncertainty.

The four problems we have just canvassed, two arising from the veil of ignorance and two from the new version of the difference principle, are handled by Rawls through a series of major revisions, additions, and alterations, whose result is a distinctively new form of the model.

[21] It is not open to Rawls to protest that calculations of the sort I have imagined are beyond the power of the most sophisticated econometric model. That is true, but it is equally true of the sorts of calculations called for by his principle.

VIII

The Third Form of the Model

AS we have seen, the veil of ignorance and the new version of the difference principle posed four problems for Rawls: first, it was not clear what, if anything, the players in the original position were to be thought to know about their world; second, it was not clear how they could engage in rational deliberation in the absence of any conception of their purposes or interests; third, the scope of application of the principles on which they were deciding was somewhat ill-defined; and, finally, the apparently counterintuitive implications of the new difference principle called for some rather more adequate account of the principles of rational choice to which they could be expected to appeal. In response to these four problems, Rawls sets out a series of theoretical elaborations that, taken all together, bring us very close to the full-scale version of the theory as it appears in *A Theory of Justice*.

The "parties" in the original position turn out to know a good deal, although not about themselves in particular. (At this point, Rawls ceases to refer to the persons in the original position as "players" in a bargaining game. The game has, so to speak, been called on account of ignorance.) The one thing in particular that they do know is that "their society is subject to the circumstances of justice," which is to say moderate scarcity, rough equality of power, and so forth. It is not clear why they need to know that their society is one in which the question of justice will arise. It would appear to be sufficient for them to ask what principles they would choose if their society were of such a nature. But the point is not significant, save as an indication of the degree to which Rawls continues to keep alive the image of a bargaining game even after he has denied the presuppositions that give logical bite to that notion.

What *is* important, however, is that the parties "know the general facts about human society" (137).[22] According to Rawls, "they understand political affairs and the principles of economic theory; they know the basis of social organization and the laws of human psychology" (137).

In Part Four, I shall suggest some reasons for believing that Rawls's hypothesis is impossible. The parties could not in principle possess all and only the knowledge Rawls imputes to them. What is more, the impossibility is logical, not merely genetic. But it is clear enough what Rawls is driving at. The parties in the original position are to be imagined as analogous to entities in a physical system who know that they possess mass, are at a position, and are (or are not) moving relative to the system with some definite speed in some definite direction; and who know the laws of motion governing the system, including themselves; but who do not know what their mass, position, and velocity in fact is, and hence can infer nothing in particular about their physical characteristics. Knowing all this, they would be able to infer any number of hypothetical propositions, of the form "If I have mass m at position p and am moving relative to the system with velocity v, and if I collide with another mass m', etc., then I will, after the collision, be traveling with velocity v', etc."

Unfortunately for Rawls, even if nonspecific knowledge of this sort about society were in principle possible,

---

[22] From this point forward, parenthetical references are to *A Theory of Justice*.

it would be very hard at this point in the development of the social sciences to say what it would consist of. What are the principles of economic theory? The neo-classical orthodoxy? Before or after the capital controversy? With or without pseudoproduction functions? Is it a "principle of economic theory," or just an odd fact, that the capital-output ratio in modern industrial economies varies very little from the figure 3:1? What counts as "the basis of social organization"? Merely a few, very general truths about the need for functional differentiation and integration, or something with more bite to it, such as Michels's iron law of oligarchy? As for the "laws of human psychology," to which Rawls appeals again and again in the later stages of the development of his full theory, their status is very uncertain indeed. Piaget would, I imagine, be happy to have his theories of cognitive development elevated to the status of laws; Erik Erikson might feel a saving embarrassment at attempts to treat his conception of the life cycle in such a manner; but Freud would surely have resisted any suggestion that the ceaseless quest for the unconscious could be transformed into a set of theoretical laws whose meaning could be known in abstraction from the particularities of the life of the knower!

At all events, the parties in the original position "are presumed to know whatever general facts affect the choice of the principles of justice." They are not yet ready to begin their deliberations, however, for as yet they know nothing about their reasons for deliberating. In order to apply the principles of prudential reason to the choice problem before them, they must assume something, however minimal, about their purpose in seeking a solution. In order to flesh out the choice situation of the parties sufficiently to get them going, deliberatively speaking, Rawls makes two further assumptions, each very powerful and highly debatable.

To begin with, Rawls imputes to each party the general knowledge that rational human beings, insofar as they *are* rational, formulate or at least act as though they have formulated what can be called "life-plans." He introduces the notion early in his exposition of the principles of justice, and returns to it much later on as part of the more general discussion of Goodness as Rationality. The following passage captures the idea quite well:

> The main idea is that a person's good is determined by what is for him the most rational long-term plan of life given reasonably favorable circumstances. A man is happy when he is more or less successful in the way of carrying out this plan. To put it briefly, the good is the satisfaction of rational desire. We are to suppose, then, that each individual has a rational plan of life drawn up subject to the conditions that confront him.

> This plan is designed to permit the harmonious satisfaction of his interests. It schedules activities so that various desires can be fulfilled without interference. It is arrived at by rejecting other plans that are either less likely to succeed or do not provide for such an inclusive attainment of aims. [92–93]

The parties in the original position can be thought to suffer from the exact opposite of the incapacity that afflicts most of us when we confront the basic choices in life. By and large, we know what we want but we do not know how to get it. They, however, know how to get whatever they want, but they do not know what they want.

As Rawls notes, the conception of a rational plan of life, in one version or another, has a long and honored philosophical heritage. My own view is that it is fundamentally wrong, for reasons I shall sketch in Part Four, but given its lineage, Rawls can hardly be faulted for leaning upon it when he must. And, as Rawls notes in the sentence preceding the passage just quoted, the notion of a rational plan of life "is not in dispute between the contract doctrine and utilitarianism" (92).

But the bare knowledge that one has a rational plan of life is not yet enough to yield a basis for rational choice among principles of distribution, for the mere fact of having such a plan tells one nothing about its relationship to the sorts of things that get distributed. Under at least some otherworldly, religiously based "plans of life" (if one could call them that), nothing within the power of men to distribute could possibly have the slightest value, up to and including physical safety and life itself. Jesus did not, after all, say to the rich young man, "Go thy way, sell whatsoever thou hast, and give to the poor, and thou shalt have treasure in heaven: and come, take up the Cross, and follow me, *but keep enough to permit you to pursue a rational plan of life.*" To a true Christian, the only distributable good worth receiving is grace, and that comes from God, not from society.

So Rawls assumes that the circumstances of justice include a secular orientation (even though, rather oddly, they seem to require, of all things, religious toleration), and lays down his theory of *primary goods*. "The primary social goods, to give them in broad categories, are rights and liberties, opportunities and powers, income and wealth" (92). The point of this "thin theory" of primary goods immediately becomes apparent when Rawls tells us that they are the sorts of things that any rational person will want more rather than less of, whatever the particularities of his life-plan. Suitably indexed (since they are multidimensional), primary goods can be treated as a quantity for which any rational agent has positive marginal utility.

Rawls makes the further stipulation that only the index of primary goods is to be taken into account in evaluating the condition of a representative man in a system of social institutions, and now the point of these maneuvers becomes clear. When the veil of ignorance was lowered, the contracting parties were deprived of all grounds for preferring one set of institutional arrangements over another. In the absence of any information about their interests and the necessary means for pursuing them, they could not even assume the minimal sort of generalized positive marginal utility (for whatever was being handed out) that would justify adoption of a strong-Pareto-preference quasi-ordering. For all they might know, in real life they might prefer less to more. But with a rational plan of life, and with the knowledge that certain primary goods are means to any such plan, they are in a position once again to take up the choice problem with some hope of solving it. It remains to be seen whether they would choose the least advantaged version of the difference principle under these now rather complicated conditions, but at least some meaning can be given to the principle. In the terms we have just introduced, it becomes the injunction to maximize the index of primary goods of the least advantaged representative man in the society.

Rawls claims that the veil of ignorance makes his problem soluble. "The veil of ignorance makes possible a unanimous choice of a particular conception of justice. Without these limitations on knowledge the bargaining problem of the original position would be hopelessly complicated" (140). It should now be clear that the truth is exactly opposite. The imposition of the veil of ignorance makes the bargaining problem hopelessly indeterminate, and hence quite insoluble. Even to get the question back into the shape of a *problem*, and not merely a shrug of the shoulders, Rawls must attribute a full knowledge of the "general facts of human society" to the parties, assume that they all have rational plans of life, add a strong theory of primary goods, and finally stipulate that the parties select their principles of distribution with only primary goods distribution in mind. Every one of these additions to the model is open to powerful objections, and it is a sign of the weakness of the veil of ignorance, not of its strength, that they are needed in order to get the theory off the ground.

In addition to the changes forced on the theory by the implications of the veil of ignorance, there are also some clarifications, revisions, and elaborations required by the new difference principle. First of all, Rawls makes it explicitly clear that the principle is to apply to the broad, basic organization or institutional arrangement of a society, not to every baseball team, stamp club, and mom-and-pop grocery store.

A society, according to Rawls, "is a more or less self-sufficient association of persons who in their relations to one another recognize certain rules of conduct as binding and who for the most part act in accordance with them. . . . (F)urther . . . these rules specify a system of cooperation designed to advance the good of those taking part in it" (4). It is not entirely clear how Rawls means us to take this definition. In order to see the problem it poses, we may recall the remarks that Max Weber addressed to the analogous task of defining the state. In the opening paragraphs of his lecture, "Politics as a Vocation," Weber observed:

> Sociologically, the state cannot be defined in terms of its ends. There is scarcely any task that some political association has not taken in hand, and there is no task that one could say has always been exclusive and peculiar to those associations which are designated as political ones: today the state, or historically, those associations which have been the predecessors of the modern state. Ultimately,

one can define the modern state sociologically only in terms of the specific *means* peculiar to it, as to every political association, namely, the use of physical force.[23]

The point is that, if we define the state in terms of its characteristic end or purpose, we shall be forced to conclude that seemingly political associations that fail to pursue that end are not merely bad states but are not states at all. In his definition of a society, Rawls goes beyond the condition of functional differentiation and integration of productive and distributive activities to require that these activities be governed by rules that specify a system of cooperation *designed* to advance the good of those taking part in it. The natural inference to draw from this definition is that the antebellum South, for example, could not be considered a *society* unless, at the very least, it could be shown that slavery constituted a system of cooperation suited to advance the interests of those (including slaves) taking part in it, and more strictly, that it was *designed* for that purpose (no latent as opposed to manifest purposes permitted).

Now, in matters of definition, the author is king, so Rawls is free to use the term "society" in this way. But since he manifestly wishes to say of many repressive "societies" that they were *unjust societies*, it would surely have been wiser for him to employ a definition that would permit him to treat such human groupings as societies. The alternative is to insist that only human groupings meeting his definition are societies, and then to add as a further premise the assumption that the parties in the original position desire to find themselves in a "society," when the veil of ignorance is lifted, rather than in some other human setting.

[23] *From Max Weber: Essays in Sociology*, trans., ed., and with an introduction by H. H. Gerth and C. Wright Mills (Oxford University Press, 1958), pp. 77–78.

Since Rawls is undoubtedly aware of Max Weber's observations and the general problem of definition we have raised, it is natural to assume that he had some good reason for building a notion of cooperative advancement of the good into his definition of society. But I confess I do not see it. What is more, Rawls reinforces the impression that he meant his definition to be value-neutral by immediately introducing the more specific concept of a "well-ordered society." A society will be called well-ordered, he stipulates, "when it is not only designed to advance the good of its members but when it is also effectively regulated by a public conception of justice" (pp. 4–5). This in turn is explained to mean a society "in which (1) everyone accepts and knows that the others accept the same principles of justice, and (2) the basic social institutions generally satisfy and are generally known to satisfy these principles" (4).

At the most elementary level, the concept of a well-ordered society is a generalization of one of the procedural implications of the original bargaining game. In its earliest form, we may recall, the players in the game were ordinary rational persons, fully aware of their individual characteristics and of the society in which they lived, and also (though Rawls does not say this explicitly) fully aware of the identities and social roles of the other "players." The rules of the bargaining game guaranteed that each player would know, completely and consciously, the precise formulation of whatever set of principles emerged from the game as its solution. What is more, the rationality and unanimity conditions guaranteed that each player would know that each other player possessed the same information. Finally, the self-interest condition ensured that any system of social differentiation and integration conforming to the principles chosen by the players would be plausibly describable as "a system of cooperation designed to advance the good of those taking part in it." Now that the veil of ignorance has been lowered and the bargaining-game character of the original position has been destroyed, Rawls must introduce as stipulations what originally followed as strict implications from the premises of the model.

At a somewhat deeper level, the assumption of a well-ordered society is designed to permit Rawls to rule out certain sorts of tricky, "noble lie" versions of utilitarianism. For example, some defenders of the principle of utility have suggested that it is actually desirable, from a utilitarian point of view, for all or most of the members of a society to hold non-utilitarian beliefs about justice, beliefs whose rigid commitment to inflexible principle is incompatible with the utilitarian expendability of general rules. Such philosophers might even agree that it would serve the purpose of utility maximization to have Rawls's theory gain universal acceptance, false though it be (they would privately insist) as a theory of justice. To this, Rawls replies that the requirement of well-ordering rules out any such Grand Inquisitorial double-dealing (454 note).

At the deepest level, I think, the idealist definition of society, as we may call it, and the further stipulation of well-ordering, express Rawls's profound commitment to the vision of a stable society in which justice and goodness are congruent.

With the entire society as his object of investigation, Rawls takes its "basic structure" as the pattern, or set of arrangements, to which the difference principle shall be applied. "Or more exactly," he says, "the way in which the major social institutions distribute fundamental rights and duties and determine the division of advantages from social cooperation" (7). In anticipation of his differentiation between political and economic arrangements, which we shall not add to this analysis until the next section, Rawls identifies the major institutions as the political constitution and the principal social and economic arrangements. He then cites, as examples of such major institutions, "the legal protection of freedom of thought and liberty of conscience, competitive markets, private property in the means of production, and the monogamous family" (4).[24]

Somewhat later, however, in the section entitled "Relevant Social Positions," Rawls simplifies his analysis considerably by stipulating that "for the most part each person holds two relevant positions: that of equal citizenship and that defined by his place in the distribution of income and wealth" (96). Once he has introduced the rule of the priority of liberty, his two principles will simply require that everyone be guaranteed secure membership in the first of these social roles and that, subject to this constraint, the expectation of the representative occupant of the least advantaged "place in the distribution of income and wealth" be maximized. Rawls can hardly help making this simplification, given the logical tasks he has set himself and considering the sort of social theory he seems willing to invoke in its aid. Were he to take seriously the notion that such disparate social institutions as monogamous marriage and private ownership of the means of production were to be treated as "major social institutions," he would have an impossible ordering problem coupled with an insoluble indexing problem. The ordering problem would arise because each individual occupies places in a number of different major social institutions, and it would be unclear which

[24] He is not endorsing private ownership of the means of production or the monogamous family, although one gets the sense that he approves of both. He is merely offering them as examples of major institutions.

81

of them to select as *the* place in terms of which to determine his ranking in the social hierarchy. The indexing problem would arise when one sought to compare the condition of the representative wife in the institution of monogamous marriage with that of the representative unskilled laborer in the institution of industrial production. But although Rawls had, in effect, no choice, he did not succeed in protecting himself from some very serious objections, as we shall see in Part Four.

Finally, with the veil of ignorance lowered, a knowledge of basic facts secured, life-plans in place, primary goods the target, major social institutions the subject of deliberation, a well-ordered society required, and the choice narrowed to principles specifying different rules for defining assignments to places in the distribution of income and wealth, Rawls must still say something persuasive about the principles of rational choice to which the parties in the original position will appeal. It is at this point in the development of the theory that a formal defense of the maximin rule of choice under uncertainty is introduced.[25]

Rawls's argument for the maximin rule is complex, and its logical status is not entirely clear. Sometimes he seems to be claiming that it is a rule that rational agents as such would consider it wise to adopt, when deliberating from a "Kantian" point of view (more of that notion later); but at other times he says that he has adjusted his characterization of the original position in order to ensure that it will be one in which the maximin rule is cho-

[25] Once again, let me remind the reader that this essay is a reconstruction of Rawls's philosophical development, not a history of it. For all I know, the arguments about maximin were among the first to enter Rawls's mind, a quarter of a century ago. My purpose in introducing them at this point is to show their logical role in his theory and to make clear what the problems are that require them here rather than at some earlier stage.

sen. The subject will receive a detailed treatment in Part Four. Here it will suffice to summarize briefly Rawls's three reasons for claiming that the parties in his original position would opt for maximin. First, he suggests, the rule is suited to cases in which "a knowledge of likelihoods is impossible, or at best extremely insecure" (154). Second, it is a rule suited to cases in which the reasoner places very little store by the additional increments he might obtain above the minimum that he can guarantee for himself by maximizing that minimum. And third, it is a suitable rule for cases in which the threatened losses below that guaranteed minimum are weighed very heavily by the reasoner. The veil of ignorance is intended to make calculations of probabilities impossible (particularly since such calculations would have to combine estimates and evaluations of all possible alternative practices with independent estimates of the likelihood of ending up in each representative role of each such practice). The theory of primary goods, together with the principle of the priority of liberty (not yet introduced into our analysis), is thought by Rawls to reduce the value of obtainable increments above the minimum. And the danger of a real insufficiency of primary goods is supposed to make unacceptable the risk of outcomes below that minimum guaranteed by the difference principle.

All the major features of Rawls's final theory are now in place, save for the priority of liberty. (Stipulations concerning the rate of savings, and other such matters, are in my view not central to the theory, although they are certainly major problems for social philosophy.) We are not yet ready to subject this theory to a systematic critique, but we have almost reached the end of the process of development. With several exceptions, the objections that now become relevant are objections *to*

Rawls's theory as such, not problems in earlier versions that led Rawls to alter or adjust the theory. There is, however, one blanket reply that Rawls can make, and indeed does make, to objections of the sort that I shall be advancing, namely that they fall before the integrated wholeness of the theory. This question of wholeness, and the legitimacy of invoking it as a justification for particular elements of the theory, concerns the logical status of the claims made throughout the book. My discussion of it is postponed until near the end of this essay, when I shall address myself directly to Rawls's notion of "reflective equilibrium."

IX

*The Priority of Liberty and
Other Complications*

AS a reader of Rawls knows, there is still an enormous number of further qualifications to add before we have the complete theory before us. I shall omit discussion of most of that material for reasons that have already been indicated. But there are several matters that do require some treatment or that raise interesting problems. Most important, clearly, is Rawls's claim that parties in the original position would choose to make the first principle, concerning equal liberty, lexically prior to the second principle, which specifies the rules of distribution. In this section, the priority of liberty and several lesser matters will be taken up. In Part Three, which follows this section, we shall explore the relationship between Kant and Rawls in a way that will, I hope, further illuminate the relation of liberty to distribution.

THE PRIORITY OF LIBERTY[26]

In the original model of the bargaining game, as we have seen, the goal of the deliberations is a set of principles for evaluating particular practices. Although Rawls does not say so, and even says some things apparently to the

---

[26] Many of my remarks on the priority of liberty follow very closely the line of argument developed by H.L.A. Hart in his essay, "Rawls on Liberty and its Priority," published originally in *University of Chicago Law Review*, Vol. 40, No. 3 (Spring, 1973), pp. 534–55, and reprinted in *Reading Rawls*, edited by Norman Daniels. See especially, Section III, "Limiting Liberty for the Sake of Liberty."

contrary, the clear implication is that certain background conditions, roughly what would be called the conditions of constitutional democracy, either are presupposed or else are built into the structure of the game itself. Just as the free market is thought to rest, in classical economic theory, on a foundation of political liberties and legal protections that guarantee each person's right to enter into contracts, to exact compliance with contracts or compensation for breaches of contract, and so forth, so Rawls's presentation of his model seems to me unmistakably to posit some such system of political rights and protections as the context of the bargaining game.

Nevertheless, from the very first, Rawls is at least ambivalent about the relation of his economic principle of justified inequality of distribution to the political principles and institutions of equal citizenship. This ambivalence appears, as I have noted, in the first formulation of the first principle of justice, which speaks of "the most extensive liberty" even though the context of the exposition makes clear that Rawls means "the largest bundle of goods and services."

With the shift in focus from micro-economic practices to macro-social institutions, and with the lowering of the veil of ignorance, Rawls reconstructs his two principles so that the first becomes a political principle of equal citizenship and the second incorporates the entire notion of justifiable deviations from equal economic distribution. Speaking historically and extrasystematically, we might say that, in the revised form of the two principles, Principle I enunciates the essence of the system of legal and political equality that developed in the late eighteenth and nineteenth centuries as the framework for the unfettered operations of industrial capitalism, and Principle II defines the standards of social justice to be used in mitigating the inequalities and hardships of those operations.

When Rawls comes to the theory of primary goods, he lists "rights and liberties, opportunities and powers, income and wealth" (90). In what he calls the simpler conception of justice, we are to imagine an index of this disparate bundle of "goods," such that we can establish at least an ordinal ranking of alternative bundles and then maximize the index assigned the least advantaged representative man.[27] Subsequently, he partitions the set of primary goods into two subsets: rights and liberties, and the rest. He then imposes a priority rule on Principles I and II whose effect is to require us to maximize the index of rights and liberties before turning our attention to the maximization of opportunities and powers, income and wealth. In the very last revision of the principles, Rawls allows a society in the earlier stages of its social and economic development to abrogate the priority rule and sacrifice some measure of liberty for a sufficient improvement in material well-being, but only in order to advance toward the time when the full rigor of the priority rule can be imposed. The net effect of the priority rule, as Rawls explains it, is to permit limitations on liberty only for the sake of liberty itself.

It is easy enough to understand why Rawls moved to the revised version of his principles of justice, despite the complexities that the revisions introduce into the

[27] The theory is problematic enough without worrying about distinctions between ordinal and cardinal measures of primary goods, but one ought to remember that, with only an ordinal ranking, no calculations of expected value of the index in risky situations can even be contemplated. In view of the ignorance of the parties in the original position, such considerations might be thought to be ruled out anyway, but the parties might wish to make calculations using conditional probabilities based on their knowledge of the basic facts of human society. They might also wish to make such calculations in the second, third, or fourth stages of the lifting of the veil. An ordinal index would make choice under risk, at any stage, impossible. When we discuss Rawls's arguments for maximin, we shall see that they presuppose cardinal utility functions.

theory. In the first place, the priority of liberty articulates Rawls's obviously deep conviction that the mutual respect of equal citizenship expresses men's recognition of one another's moral personality. It is, as we shall see, Rawls's way of embodying in his theory the Kantian injunction to treat humanity, whether in oneself or others, always as an end and never merely as a means. To bargain away a portion of one's liberties for a softer life would, in Rawls's view, be to sell one's birthright as a human being for a mess of potage.

At the same time, Rawls's use of quasi-economic models of reasoning makes it extremely difficult to aggregate political and economic considerations into a single measure or "index." By partitioning the set of primary goods and imposing a priority rule, Rawls is able to separate essentially political questions of legal statuses, constitutional guarantees, and governmental forms from economic questions of the structure of the work world, the operations of the market, and the distribution of income and status. It is for this reason, among others, that Rawls settles on just two relevant positions for each person in the basic structure of a society. The first, equal citizenship, corresponds to the principle of equal liberty; the second, one's place in the distribution of income and wealth, corresponds to the difference principle.

Finally, the qualification that the priority rule comes into play only above some decent minimum level of welfare is required in order to rule out manifestly absurd judgments. If strict priority were observed, then not even a catastrophic decline in the index of primary goods, bad enough to threaten the extinction of the society, would be permitted to justify the slightest relaxation of the formal, constitutional equal liberty with which the society advanced to its doom, even though there might be every reason to suppose that survival could be purchased at the price of temporary tyranny.

What are we to make of the principle of the priority of liberty? Leaving to one side the question of its ultimate truth and also any consideration of its conformity to one or another person's moral intuitions, let us simply ask two questions: first, does the principle make sense, can we understand what it means and how it would be applied; and, second, would the parties in the original position choose it?

A bit more than halfway through *A Theory of Justice*, Rawls finally states his two principles in their final form, complete with priority rules. Here is the portion relevant to our discussion:

First Principle
Each person is to have an equal right to the most extensive total system of equal basic liberties compatible with a similar system of liberty for all.

. . . .

First Priority Rule (The Priority of Liberty)
The principles of justice are to be ranked in lexical order and therefore liberty can be restricted only for the sake of liberty. There are two cases:
  (a) a less extensive liberty must strengthen the total system of liberty shared by all;
  (b) a less than equal liberty must be acceptable to those with the lesser liberty. [302]

Rawls has obviously simplified his indexing problem by separating rights and liberties from opportunities and powers, income and wealth, in the class of primary goods. But since he adheres to a quasi-economic maximization model, he is still required by the form of his principle to appeal to some indexing procedure for liberties. If one were simply elaborating formal models, a first step might be a multidimensional analysis of liberty and the invocation of a unanimity quasi-ordering. Any change in an individual's basic liberties that diminished his liberty along no dimension and increased his liberty along at least one dimension would be a positive change; and so forth. Then one would have to face the problems of aggregation, or indexing, in order to arrive at a complete ordering sufficient to say whether any one total system of basic liberties was more extensive, less extensive, or equally as extensive as any other total system. As H.L.A. Hart argues with great persuasiveness in the essay cited at the beginning of this section, such rankings and comparisons within the realm of political and legal liberty are very far from being easy. Many of the most deep-seated and intractable political disagreements among conscientious and honorable citizens take precisely the form of diametrically opposed judgments of the acceptability of limiting one freedom for the sake of another.

But there is, it seems to me, a still deeper problem, arising out of the economic ancestry of Rawls's equal liberty principle. I can understand, historically as well as institutionally, what it means to say that in a political system all men are equal before the law. That phrase conjures up the demand that all persons be accountable before a single tribunal, that there not be ecclesiastical courts for the clergy, or a House of Lords for peers. I can understand too the principle of political equality, as it translates into universal suffrage, the universal right to hold political office, and so forth. But I have very great difficulty formulating a usable notion of a *measure* of liberty, in terms of which I could judge whether a given system of laws permitted a larger or smaller amount of, say, freedom of speech.

At the risk of appearing facetious, let me pose some simple, even simple-minded, questions. Does greater freedom of speech mean freedom to speak more often, or

to more people, or about more important subjects? Does
it mean freedom to deviate more widely from the socially
accepted canon of permitted opinions? Merely to ask
questions of this nature is to make it obvious that one is
thinking of the subject in the wrong way. And yet, I do
not see how Rawls can avoid subjecting himself to such
inquiries, once he adopts the formula of "the most extensive liberty compatible with a like liberty for all."

To objections of this nature, Rawls has two answers.
The first, which is rather elegant, is the distinction between liberty and the worth of liberty (204). This permits
him to get round the familiar jibe that under capitalist
democracy the poor man and the rich man have the same
legal right to buy a meal at an expensive restaurant. But
the indexing problem does not arise because equal liberties are of unequal worth to persons at different levels in
the hierarchy of opportunities and powers, income and
wealth. It arises because of the necessity of ordering different degrees of liberty and then aggregating quanta of
liberties of different sorts into a single measure of the
magnitude of a total system of liberty. Rawls's real answer to the problem is simply to retreat to his moral intuitions, reminding the reader that there are limits to
the precision that can be achieved by any moral theory.
But a retreat to intuition is an acceptable manuever only
when one is tidying up the boundaries of a moral theory.
As Hart points out, however, our uncertainties occur in
the very heartland of the domain of political liberty.
Rawls simply does not explain what his principle *means*
when it speaks of "the most extensive liberty." The answer to our first question is therefore, no: we cannot understand what the principle means and how it would be
applied.

Would the parties in the original position choose the
first principle, as part of their solution to the rational

choice problem before them? And would they attach to it the extremely strong priority rule enunciated by Rawls? Under the interpretation of the original position so strongly suggested by the early formulations of Rawls's theory, and carried over into the language and reasoning of *A Theory of Justice*, the answer seems to me to be a qualified no. But a stronger case can be made for the priority of equal liberty under the Kantian interpretation of the original position, and it is for that reason, I surmise, that the section on the Kantian interpretation immediately follows the section entitled "The Priority of Liberty Defined."

The source of the difficulty is the notion of a plan of life, as Rawls invokes it to give structure to the choice problem in the original position. *A Theory of Justice*, as a manifesto of a political faith, stands in the great tradition reaching back to Aristotle's *Politics* of the celebration of the *polis*, the community of rational agents who find their highest good and their most complete fulfillment in the rational discourse and collective deliberation by which they manage their common affairs. It is this vision of the just society as the end, not merely a means, of life that inspires Rousseau to write:

> The better a state is constituted, the more do public affairs intrude upon private affairs in the minds of the citizens. Private concerns even become considerably fewer, because each individual shares so largely in the common happiness that he has not so much occasion to seek for it in private resources. [28]

I myself find this vision of the just society inspiring, though I admit to considerable ambivalence about the loss of privacy and intrusiveness it implies. And a party in the original position who knew that such a vision in-

[28] *The Social Contract*, Book III, Chapter XV.

formed his plan of life would very likely opt for a Rawlsian principle of the most extensive equal liberty, if he could make sense of it, complete with a strong form of the priority rule. But there are other plans of life, equally rational by any but the most loaded conception of rationality, in which political liberty is merely a means to private ends, not one of the principal ends itself. To persons with such plans of life, trade-offs between liberty and income would be quite appealing, at least within fairly broad limits designed to protect one from the most serious constrictions of rights. Knowing only that they had rational plans of life, and even knowing that the successful execution of those plans would require primary goods (the more the better), parties in the original position could have no way of knowing whether their plans of life were such as to justify a strong emphasis on liberty as opposed to income, and no reason at all to opt for an absolute lexical ordering of the two subclasses of primary goods.

In order to establish so powerful a conclusion, Rawls must find some way of showing that merely to be a rational moral agent entails ranking the liberties of a democratic political order absolutely above income and wealth, at least once a decent minimum has been secured. Rawls finds such an argument in the Kantian interpretation of the original position.

OTHER COMPLICATIONS

Even after making all the adjustments to the model of the preceding stages, Rawls realizes that he does not yet have the materials for a theorem, and so he introduces a few additional complications. Since the purpose of this essay is to lay bare the underlying structure of the development of Rawls's theory, rather than to comment upon it *seriatim*, I shall not try to follow all the twists and turns of the exposition. Nevertheless, a few points call for some comment.

Strictly speaking, with regard to the problem of rational choice as it is posed in the original position, Rawls ought to define a bargaining space of possible solution points and then present arguments to show that the players would settle upon a single point, or set of points, in that space. In the original form of the model, the "solutions" were principles of division of a bundle of commodities, and the homogeneity of the problem seemed to offer hope that one could define such a solution space. But in the final version, the alternatives among which the parties must choose are really nothing less than total social philosophies, and there is no clear way of identifying the dimensions along which such philosophies can vary so as to define a space of available solutions. As a consequence, Rawls substitutes a much simplified version of the choice problem for the one originally conceived, by stipulating that the parties shall be presented with a limited list of alternatives from which to choose. (See Section 21.) The alternatives presented to the parties in the original position are, essentially, various forms of utilitarianism, certain intuitionist doctrines, Rawls's own two principles of justice, and a few of the more plausible mixtures of these.

Rawls is quite aware of the unsatisfactory nature of this simplification. As he says, "admittedly this is an unsatisfactory way to proceed" (123). But I think it is fair to say that the drawbacks of the procedure do not trouble him greatly, because, as I suggested in my opening remarks, he is really engaged in a dispute with intuitionism and utilitarianism. There is nothing unusual or reprehensible in a philosopher concentrating his attention on what he conceives to be his main philosophical competitors and ignoring other alternatives, but such narrowing of focus considerably undermines the claim to be considering the issues *sub specie aeternitatis*.

We have already noted the restriction on the priority of liberty—it is to take effect only after a sufficient level of material well-being is reached in the society. Rawls adds a further qualification to his full-scale statement of the two principles to the effect that a just rate of savings shall be adopted by the society as a whole.

Despite the economic sophistication of his discussion, Rawls's treatment of the subject of an appropriate rate of savings can hardly be called a success. The problem does not lie so much with his conclusions as with the subject itself. There simply does not seem to be any reasonable answer to the question: How much ought this generation to sacrifice for the well-being of future generations? The question, heaven knows, is real enough. Indeed, in countries that combine a low level of economic development with a high degree of centralization of decision making, it is probably the most important single question that the government can put to itself and its economic advisers. But if I may intrude my own moral intuitions into the analysis, I find on reflection that I cannot get even a rough fix on an answer by focusing on considerations of justice.

Now, when a problem of fundamental importance in moral or social philosophy seems utterly resistant to enlightenment from a particular point of view, it may be a signal that the point of view is all wrong. I should like to sketch a few remarks designed to suggest that the problem of a just rate of savings exposes a very deep inadequacy in the basic philosophical orientation of Rawls, and also, I might add, of the utilitarian, intuitionist, and social contract traditions as well.

The particular difficulty of choosing a rate of savings

originates in the fact that the parties do not know which generation of their own society they come from. Remember that, in Rawls's model, their task is not to select a *just* rate of savings, but just to *select* a rate of savings that is, under the peculiar knowledge constraints of their situation, rationally self-interested. The whole point of the original position is supposed to be that, by virtue of the pure procedural justice of the situation, whatever choice they make *will* be just. To save nothing for even the very next generation seems manifestly unwise; to save everything one possibly can over many generations, so that the last generations of the society can live in total comfort, seems equally imprudent. And to strike a balance between the two has all the appearance of an ad hoc resolution of an insoluble dilemma. To be sure, considerations of efficiency and declining marginal productivity may narrow the scope of feasible alternatives somewhat, but not in a manner to transform the problem into one of rational choice.

If we try to imagine real-world versions of the dilemma, we can see why neither justice nor rational choice lies at the heart of the problem. Should the Chinese people sacrifice a generation, in effect, by the most severe bearable constraints on consumption in order to maximize the rate of capital accumulation for the sake of future generations? Or should they adopt a slower rate of growth so that those now living and working can enjoy some of the fruits of their labor before they are too old? That is not a question to which there is a correct moral answer. We may agree that their choice, whatever it should be, must be theirs and not that of their rulers. But if as a people they should freely choose to sacrifice for coming generations, could we plausibly say that they had acted unjustly? And if, on the contrary, they should choose to enjoy some modest rise in their standard of living while expanding their industrial plant more slowly, could we plausibly call *that* choice unjust?

The source of this difficulty is the way in which Rawls would have us look at the question. Rawls conceives of the moral point of view as an atemporal vantage from which, like Lucretius gazing down upon the plain of battle, we contemplate all time and all space equanimously and isotropically. So the choice of a rate of savings, made by one generation for all generations, is formally identical with a choice made by one proper subset of all of the rational agents at a given time for all of the rational agents at that time. The fact that those not included in the choosing come at a later time (or have come at an earlier time) is to be treated no differently from the fact that those not included in some act of choice are located at a different place from those who are included.

But human existence is not accidentally temporal; it is essentially temporal. What makes it a matter of *justice* how a subgroup chooses for the whole society is the fact that in principle the entire group *could* be included in the choosing. What makes it seem a matter of justice how parents choose for their children is the human fact that generations overlap, so that the children, the parents, and the grandparents must live for a time in the same world. What makes it manifestly *not* a matter of justice how this generation chooses for a generation far in the future is the certainty that they cannot share the same world, and hence could not even in principle gather together to share the act of choice.

The veil of ignorance creates a choice situation in which the *essential* characteristics of human existence are set aside along with accidents of individual variation. What results, it seems to me, is not a moral point of view, but a nonhuman point of view from the perspective of which moral questions are not clarified but warped and distorted.

Very little needs to be said about such details as the

four-stage lifting of the veil of ignorance. Systematic philosophers have the habit of fleshing out the skeletons of their theories with elaborations whose logical relationship to the theory itself might be described as one of possibility rather than actuality or necessity. When Hobbes permutes and combines the elements of his theory of psychological egoism to generate a series of brilliant definitions of character predicates, when Kant manages to slip into the empty pigeon-holes of his architectonic his own particular dynamical theory of matter, we must not imagine that these are deductions from the first premises of the *Leviathan* or the *Critique*. We cannot even suppose that the central theories of those works lend any special credence to the subsidiary materials that have filled them out. Rather, Hobbes and Kant (and countless other systematic philosophers as well) are merely showing that their theories have room for, will admit, can find a neat place for, some bit of psychologizing or moralizing or scientific speculating to which they are very much attached.

I think we can take a similar view of a great deal of the elaboration that lengthens, but does not deepen, *A Theory of Justice*. I realize that Rawls will disagree most vehemently with this assessment, but the plain fact is that, in my judgment, the book would have been stronger and more persuasive without the lengthy disquisitions on stability and congruence, without the detail of the four-stage veil-lifting and even without the discussions of moral psychology.

PART THREE
RAWLS AND KANT

X

Kant and Rawls

WHEN Rawls lowers the veil of ignorance over the players of the bargaining game in the original position, he transforms their situation so completely that it ceases to be, in any recognizable sense, a bargaining game. Indeed, Rawls asserts, as though it were one of the virtues of the veil of ignorance, that under it "the parties have no basis for bargaining in the usual sense" (139). For reasons that I shall develop in Part Four, this change seems to me to undermine the entire edifice of Rawls's theory and destroy what was the central idea of the first form of the model. Somewhat surprisingly, Rawls embraces the transformation and argues for it as one of the grounds for the general moral plausibility of his theory.

The introduction of the veil of ignorance, as we have seen, was necessitated by the simple unprovability of the theorem in its original form. But the attractiveness of the veil of ignorance pretty clearly derives from the fact that it links up Rawls's line of analysis with a quite different tradition of moral philosophy, one to which he is drawn as strongly as he is to the classical economic, Anglo-American tradition from which his models of analysis and argument come, namely the moral philosophy of Immanuel Kant.

Rawls offers an explicit "Kantian interpretation" of the original position in its final, veil-of-ignorance form, and we shall examine that interpretation shortly. But it is worth noting two other ways in which Rawls appears to echo Kant's philosophical tactics and style, the first of them quite profound, the second merely superficial. Profundity first.[29]

Kant's early philosophical work concentrated on attempts to mediate the theoretical conflict between the Leibnizean school of rationalist metaphysics and the British scientific school of Newton and his followers. His early papers took first one side and then the other in the famous dispute, but in 1770 Kant hit upon what he felt to be a satisfactory resolution of the conflict. In the *Inaugural Dissertation* presented on the occasion of his elevation to a chair at the University of Königsberg, Kant proposed in effect a compromise or fusion of the two schools. Transforming what had been a metaphysical and scientific argument into an epistemological issue, Kant argued that neither reason nor the senses is the sole source of our knowledge of objects. Reason, he claimed, gives us knowledge of things as they really are, by means of pure concepts generated out of reason's inner resources; and the senses give us knowledge of things as they appear to us, under the forms of space and time. In the *Critique of Pure Reason*, Kant gave up the claim that reason could yield a knowledge of things as they are in themselves, but he continued to describe sensibility as a limitation upon understanding. Our powers of theoretical reason alone, he said, could give us nothing save the empty tautologies of logic. But if to the pure form of theoretical reason we added the constraint of sensibility—if, that is to say, we restricted ourselves to conditionally a priori assertions concerning objects of a pos-

---

[29] In the remainder of Part Three, I shall draw heavily on my own previous studies of the philosophy of Kant. See especially *Kant's Theory of Mental Activity* (Harvard University Press, 1963) and *The Autonomy of Reason: A Commentary on Kant's Groundwork of the Metaphysic of Morals* (Harper & Row, 1973).

sible (sensible) experience in general—then we could arrive at extremely powerful, quite general conclusions. We could, in fact, establish the (conditionally) a priori validity of pure physics and pure mathematics. Although our conclusions would be limited by the constraints of the conditions of human knowledge, they would be perfectly general within that broad sphere, and they would be established entirely a priori, without appeal to particular observation or experience.

I should like to suggest that the original form of Rawls's theory is built upon a maneuver that bears a striking resemblance to this idea of Kant. In effect, we can imagine Rawls saying, the purely formal principles of practical reason, as explicated by the theory of individual rational choice, do not suffice to yield any substantive conclusions for morality. But suppose that we impose on these purely formal principles a procedural constraint. Like the constraints of pure space and time, which according to Kant "contain nothing but mere relations" (B66), the constraints of the bargaining game, including the willingness to make a commitment to principles, contain no specific details of the desires, intentions, motives, or beliefs of the players.[30] Nevertheless, Rawls says, I shall show that powerful substantive conclusions can be drawn from these apparently barren premises. In fact, he tells us, he hopes to prove *as a theorem* the proposition that rational agents, constrained in their deliberations by the procedural rules of the bargaining game in addition to the purely formal principles of practical reason, must necessarily settle upon his two principles of justice as the solution of their problem of collective rational choice. It is a powerful idea, and though it is

[30] This may help to explain why I consider it so significant a retreat for Rawls to introduce even a "thin" theory of the good into his model.

by now clear that it did not work, we can easily see why Rawls clung to it to the very last, despite the many revisions, adjustments, and concessions that transformed his original theory.

The second resemblance between Rawls and Kant is considerably less important though it is suggestive nonetheless. Kant was an inveterate system-builder. He placed great store by what he called the "architectonic" structure of his theory (see Chapter III of the Transcendental Doctrine of Method at the very end of the *Critique*), and he was forever claiming that the thorough-going unity and completeness of his system was one of the principal arguments for its truth. Rawls too has a passion for systematic wholeness. It is reflected in the repeated references forward and backward from one part of his book to another, and in the frequent injunctions not to attempt to judge the suitability of any particular element of the theory of justice without weighing its relation to all of the other elements, and to the unity of their interconnectedness.

Now the fact is that, despite Kant's absolute genius for categorization and classification, the architectonic is virtually worthless as a guide to the real philosophical heart of his theories. More often than not, the appeals to the overarching plan of the Critical Philosophy direct one away from its most important discoveries. In like manner, I suggest, Rawls's claims for systematic completeness cannot bear much philosophical weight, even though, like Kant, he would undoubtedly insist that he meant them to be taken with the utmost seriousness. Since *A Theory of Justice* is a long book, with little or no padding, and since Rawls is manifestly one of the most self-consciously sophisticated philosophers ever to write moral and political philosophy, it is easy to suppose that one has simply missed the point when some portion of his theory seems not to hold up. One of my purposes in setting forth the theory as a several-staged development, rather than as a completed whole, is to support my contention that much of the architectonic elaboration is either a sort of systemic afterthought or else a defensive response to possible objections to earlier stages.

XI

The Kantian Background

RAWLS'S explicit attempt to connect his moral theory to the philosophy of Kant is the "Kantian" interpretation that he offers of the original position in its mature, or veil-of-ignorance, form. To put the point succinctly and somewhat misleadingly, the veil of ignorance is supposed to have the effect of limiting the parties in the original position to the rational deliberations they would engage in as noumenal agents rather than as phenomenal creatures. The real relationship between Kant and Rawls is rather more complicated, and will require a bit of background to make it clear.

Kant's aim in the Critical Philosophy is to identify and isolate the a priori element in cognition and to subject it to a critique that will establish its validity. In the opening paragraphs of the *Groundwork* he somewhat simplifyingly divides all cognition into Logic, Physics, and Ethics—which is to say, into the purely formal rules of all thought in general, the principles of the theoretical use of reason, and the principles of the practical use of reason. The truths of logic achieve absolutely unconditional, universal validity by virtue of their total emptiness. They apply, as it were, to everything and to nothing. The purpose of the *Critique of Pure Reason* is to establish the a priori validity of the principles of theoretical reason—physics and mathematics—but of course Kant pays a price for this victory. Since physics and mathematics are substantive rather than purely formal, their a priori validity is conditioned rather than unconditioned. They can be known a priori to be true, on the condition that their scope of application is confined within the limits of a possible experience in general. Sensibility, as the faculty of the mind by means of which objects of cognition can be presented to consciousness, sets the limits of possible theoretical knowledge.

When he turns to the a priori principles of practical reason—to ethics—Kant deliberately shuns the line of reasoning that he employed with such success in his treatment of theoretical reason. Since the "objects" of practical reason are the ends or goals at which we aim in our action, Kant could have developed a theory of the conditionally a priori principles of practical reason, according to which the a priori validity of the principles is conditioned by their limitation to the possible ends or purposes of human agents. A theory of desire, analogous to the theory of the forms of space and time, would then have yielded a system of principles of practical reason.

Kant might have taken such a line. Had he done so, he would presumably have developed a theory much like that of Aristotle or Hume. But he was convinced that such a theory, however complex and imposing it might have been, would not be an ethical theory. At best, it would be a theory of rational prudence. It would yield conclusions whose truth was conditioned by the particular structure of desire of human beings. Just as our pure mathematics would be different, Kant held, if our form of outer intuition had been other than it is; and just as our pure physics would be different if the system of pure concepts of the understanding, or categories, had been other than what it is; so such an ethical theory would imply that our rights and duties would be different if the de facto structure of our faculty of desire were different.

The point is not that for creatures different from ourselves the concrete application of moral principles would result in different particular constellations of obligations. Kant was quite content to grant that innocuous claim.

The problem for him was that, on an ethical theory constructed along the lines of his theory of theoretical knowledge, *the moral principles themselves* would be contingent upon the particular nature of human beings. To make such a claim, Kant thought, would be quite simply to reveal that one did not understand what moral principles are!

The central problem of Kant's ethical theory, therefore, is to establish that the fundamental principles of morality have, at one and the same time, the absolutely unconditionally universal scope of the empty principles of logic and the substantive, nontrivial significance of the first principles of mathematics and physics. Much of the obscurity and confusion of Kant's ethical theory derives not from his employment of an outmoded psychological vocabulary nor from the cultural limitations of his eighteenth-century north German pietist moral convictions, but simply from the manifest difficulty, not to say impossibility, of his philosophical goal.

Kant finds the key to his dilemma, in ethics as in the rest of his philosophy, in the distinction between appearance and reality. By means of that distinction, he believes he can resolve the conflict between the freedom that is the defining mark of moral agency and the determinism that has been established for the natural world by the arguments of the *First Critique*. As a purely rational, atemporal being, a self-in-itself, I am capable of moving myself to act by the rational apprehension of the timeless laws of practical reason; I am, in short, free. As an appearance in the field of my consciousness, an object of my own theoretical reason, I am subordinated to the same system of empirical laws that orders all the phenomena of the realm of appearance.

Now, even to act prudentially in pursuit of the ends or objects set for me by my phenomenally determined system of desires, I must engage in practical reasoning of a sort not possible to merely phenomenal beings.[31] But the principles of prudential reason are conditional in their form. They assert: Having end E as your goal, do A, which is a means to E. An agent who does indeed have end E as his end will, insofar as he is rational, do A. But nothing in the analysis of prudential rationality establishes that agents, qua rational, must take certain particular ends as their ends. So Kant can say, a bit misleadingly but with the intention of connecting up his analysis of prudential reason with his analysis of pure logic, that the principle, "Who wills the end wills the means," is *analytic*.

But moral principles command categorically, not hypothetically, and Kant's problem is to discover some way of establishing the objective validity of substantive, non-empty principles whose scope of application is in no way conditional upon an agent's acknowledgment of the end posited by the principle. Kant expresses this problem somewhat misleadingly by asking how synthetic principles of pure practical reason are possible a priori.

There are actually two distinct problems intertwined in Kant's discussion of the possibility of a categorical imperative, and if we are to understand exactly how Rawls's theory does and does not resemble Kant's, we must separate them out quite clearly. The first problem, which dominates the discussion of imperatives in Chapter Two of the *Groundwork*, is how a finite, conditioned creature such as man can stand under, or be bound by,

[31] Throughout this discussion, I rely very heavily on the detailed analysis of Kant's theory in my commentary on the *Groundwork*. Since some of the assertions I make are quite controversial among students of Kant, I can only urge the reader who finds them puzzling, or who seeks further elaboration of them, to consult *The Autonomy of Reason*.

an unconditioned moral principle. Kant construes this as the task of investigating "the possibility of a *categorical* imperative," an investigation that he says must be conducted "entirely *a priori*."[32] The puzzle is how a creature whose behavior is determined by the natural causation of desire and inclination can, nevertheless, be obligated to determine its own actions by its rational apprehension of the principles of pure practical reason. These principles appear to us men as imperatives because we lack the perfect or holy will of purely rational beings.

The second problem, which motivates much of Kant's most suggestive and difficult philosophical argumentation, including the derivation of the categorical imperative in Chapters One and Two and the discussion of humanity as an end in itself, is how the purely formal principles of practical reason, akin in their empty formality to the laws of logic, can possibly yield substantive moral principles. The difficulty here is not how such finite and morally feeble creatures as ourselves can ever hope to adhere to the principles of morality, or how we can be expected to do so. The problem is how there could *be* substantive moral principles for us to adhere to, even supposing that we were perfectly rational, and hence free from the temptations of sensibility. To put the question in the terms that Kant uses as he introduces the *Groundwork*, whence come the objective *ends* that can serve as the content for the pure *form* of practical reason?

Kant offers three answers, all ultimately unsatisfactory. The first is to claim that from a purely formal principle (the categorical imperative) one can derive just those particular substantive principles that are universally binding on all rational agents as such. The famous

[32] *Kants Werke*, Ak., IV, 419–20.

application of the categorical imperative to four proposed "maxims" (concerning suicide, false promising, helping others, and developing one's natural talents) is Kant's effort—a failure—to show that the categorical imperative can rule out the wrong maxims of action and rule in the right ones. The second attempt, somewhat farther on in the same chapter, is the doctrine that humanity is an end-in-itself, and hence an end that every rational agent must take as his end. Although the discussion of the dignity of humanity is one of the most moving passages in the literature of moral philosophy, its argument cannot establish the conclusion Kant needs, which is that there is some goal or end that all rational creatures as such take for their end, and which therefore gives content to the empty formula of the categorical imperative. Kant's third and final attempt, in the *Metaphysics of Morals*, is simply to assert without argument that there are two objective or "obligatory" ends, namely the happiness of others and my own perfection.

In the end, we must conclude that Kant failed to discover a way to deduce objective, obligatory ends from the mere analysis of what it is to be a rational agent. He was therefore unable also to establish the unconditionally universal validity of any substantive principles of practical reason. My own view is that his failure was inevitable, because there are no such principles, but in any event, I am convinced that Kant's arguments do not work.

XII

The Kantian Interpretation of the Original Position[33]

A S I have pointed out, the original idea of the bargaining game among rationally self-interested agents bore a striking resemblance to Kant's notion that sensibility limits, and thereby gives significant applications to, the pure concepts of understanding. But Rawls himself chooses to find his point of contact with Kant in the revised conception of the original position as a condition of rational choice under the veil of ignorance. As he says near the end of the section devoted to the Kantian interpretation, "The original position may be viewed, then, as a procedural interpretation of Kant's conception of autonomy and the categorical imperative" (256). The idea is that, by choosing in abstraction from, or in ignorance of, our particular characteristics, abilities, and personal histories, we are choosing as though we were noumenal rather than phenomenal beings. Since each of us freely chooses the principles under whose rule he will live, each of us is a law-giver to himself and hence is autonomous. It is open to us, of course, not to adopt the point of view of the original position, but our decision to do so "expresses our nature as free and equal rational persons" (256).

Rawls's Kantian interpretation is an enormously suggestive gloss of the original position, and no brief discus-

---

[33] With this section, see the fine essay by Andrew Levine, "Rawls' Kantianism," in *Social Theory and Practice*, Vol. 3, No. 1 (Spring, 1974), pp. 47–63.

sion can do it justice. Nevertheless, I am persuaded that it is misleading in several important ways, and I think that by sketching these, we may also become clearer about what Rawls's theory does and does not accomplish.

The difficulty is that Rawls appears to have carried into his own discussion Kant's confusion about the two distinct problems posed by the doctrine of the categorical imperative. The first problem is how self-interested creatures such as ourselves can adopt and adhere to a principle of practical reason that eschews all reference to the objects of our interests. The second problem is how a purely formal principle of practical reason can yield substantive conclusions in the form of non-empty moral principles.

To be autonomous, Kant says, is to be "subject only to laws which are made by (oneself) and yet are universal" (Ak., IV, 432). A superficial reading of this and other passages makes it appear that the essence of autonomy is *self*-legislation. But if one looks more closely, it becomes clear that Kant has in mind the distinction between legislation, or willing, that is guided by and hence subservient to desire or inclination—which he labels heteronomy—and legislation or willing that ignores or abstracts from sensuous motives. Such legislating he calls autonomous. The connection between autonomy and universality is simply that when I will a principle purely in my character as a rational agent, abstracting from all particularizing sensuous content, I necessarily will the same law that would be legislated by any other rational agent in like circumstances. Since it is the content of willing, or desire, that differentiates one rational agent from another, not the pure form of practical reason, it follows that the law I will qua rational agent is the law that any rational agent as such would will, and hence is binding on all rational agents.

113

So the utilitarian who gives *to himself* the law "Act so as to produce the greatest happiness for the greatest number" is heteronomous rather than autonomous, for in his willing he takes pleasure or happiness, whether his own or another's, as the end of his action. The law he wills is therefore not binding on a rational agent who does not posit that end. At best, such a principle, although altruistic, would be a conditioned rather than an unconditioned principle, and its expression would take the form of a hypothetical rather than a categorical imperative.

Since it is as noumenal agents that we are capable of rational willing, and it is of our phenomenal character that the particularities of our spatio-temporal character can be predicated, we abstract in our role as rational agents from everything that differentiates one of us from another in the field of appearance. This is the fact that leads Rawls to associate his account of the original position with the kingdom of ends, and to say that a party in the original position is like a noumenal agent.

But when the parties in the original position are deprived of any knowledge of themselves as particular agents, they are also deprived of the basis for rational deliberation, *just as Kant's noumenal agents are.* So long as a rational agent attends only to the pure form of practical reason, he cannot possibly arrive at substantive conclusions concerning the principles of right action. The parties under a total veil of ignorance will suffer exactly the same incapacity. So Rawls first lets them know that they are rationally *self*-interested, not merely that they are rational. Since even that is not enough to permit them to come to any significant conclusions, he adds a knowledge of the basic facts of human society, a knowledge that they possess plans of life of a certain determinate structure, and a theory of primary goods as a supplement to the theory of life plans. Finally, the parties have enough, Rawls thinks, to draw some conclusions.

In Part Four, I shall argue that Rawls has given his parties too much (the knowledge of the basic facts . . .) and too little (the bare notion of a plan of life and an inadequate theory of primary goods) for the choice problem confronting them. But even if their store of knowledge were, as Goldilocks would say, just right, it still would not yield "autonomously willed" principles, in Kant's sense. What Rawls claims is that "the veil of ignorance deprives the persons in the original position of the knowledge that would enable them to choose heteronomous principles" (252), but in fact it only guarantees that their principles will be, so to speak, generally heteronomous rather than particularly heteronomous. The choice of principles is motivated by self-interest, rather than by the Idea of the Good.

The real merit of Rawls's Kantian interpretation lies in its construal of the second problem bound up with the categorical imperative—the problem of explaining how a sensuously limited creature can stand under, and be bound by, categorical principles of morality. Kant does not really have an answer, despite his elaborate metaphysical distinction between the realms of appearance and reality, and Rawls cannot be said to have an answer either, in the strict sense. Nevertheless, Rawls's notion of "expression" (255), and with it his claim that by adopting the point of view of the original position we "express our nature as free and equal rational persons" (256), does seem to me to articulate one of the central ideas of Kant's moral philosophy.

It remains true for Rawls, as it is for Kant, that he can offer no reply to the skeptic who asks, Why should I be

115

moral? But if the argument from the original position were sound in other ways, that fact would be at best a feeble objection.

Finally, we can understand the inner connection between the priority of liberty and the Kantian interpretation of the original position. The political forms demanded by the principle of equal liberty are the institutional embodiment of the collective decision to give expression to men's recognition of one another as free and equal rational persons. It is the fundamental constitutional principle of the Kingdom of Ends. Rawls errs (in my judgment) in attempting to load that principle with plans of life and a thin theory of the good. He errs too, I believe, in attempting to extract the mutual recognition of the dignity of personality from a bargaining constraint on rational self-interest. But in light of Kant's failure to arrive at satisfactory substantive conclusions on the basis of an analysis of the pure form of practical reason, the attractions of Rawls's tactic are not difficult to understand.

XIII

The General Facts about Human Society

IN Part Two, when I was attempting to exhibit Rawls's theory as the outcome of a process of development, I sketched a number of criticisms of early forms of the model and suggested that we might best understand the final theory as a response, in part, to the difficulties revealed by those criticisms. Most if not all of the difficulties were seen by Rawls himself; his development was not so much a response to critics as an inner intellectual or philosophical growth. At the end of Part Two, in my discussion of the priority of liberty and the principle of savings, I did indicate some reasons for questioning those elements of the final theory, but since they are secondary elaborations, I do not think Rawls's philosophy in any way stands or falls on their defensibility.

It is now time to consider the theory as such, and to ask whether it can be adequately defended. In the four sections of this part of the essay, I shall offer a number of arguments designed to show that Rawls's theory is unsound. In keeping with the central thesis of the essay, I shall focus principally on what I consider to be the core of the theory, namely the model of a bargaining game played under the conditions that Rawls summarizes as "the original position." In this section and the next, I will take issue with certain of the ad hoc adjustments of the original position Rawls introduced to get his bargaining game under way. Specifically, I shall argue that the knowledge conditions of the original position are impossible, that the "thin theory" of primary goods is inadequate to Rawls's needs, and that the notion of a plan of life is a distortion of the humanly rational.)

In Section XV, I shall attempt to make precise the structure of the bargaining game in order to determine whether it can plausibly be expected to issue in the "solution" claimed by Rawls. As we shall see, the answer is no, for a variety of what seem to me to be very serious reasons. Rawls is confused about what he means by "maximin"; the maximin rule of choice of strategies does not by itself yield the two principles of justice on any plausible reconstruction of the game; Rawls's invocation of what he calls "pure procedural justice" is incorrect in a way that is important and damaging for his theory; and his arguments for adopting maximin simply do not stand up.

In the final section of this part, I shall try to come to grips with the tricky issue of the logical status of Rawls's argument, with particular attention to his distinctive doctrine of "reflective equilibrium." The message of Part Four is that the core of Rawls's theory is wrong: the two principles of justice simply are not, in any sense, the solution to the sort of bargaining game sketched by Rawls.

Let us turn first to the knowledge conditions in the original position.[34] Under the veil of ignorance, a party forgets all the details of his personal life, including his talents, abilities, interests, purposes, culture, sex, age, plan of life, historical location, and so forth. So far as particulars are concerned, he knows only that outside the temple of justice awaits a situation constrained or defined by the circumstances of justice. But he retains his

[34] Among the many articles that deal with this subject, let me direct the reader's attention particularly to Benjamin Barber's unusually complex and penetrating essay, "Justifying Justice: Problems of Psychology. Politics and Measurement in Rawls," in Norman Daniels, *Reading Rawls* (Basic Books, 1975). His essay also deals with the subjects discussed in Section XV.

knowledge of the "general facts about human society." He understands "political affairs and the principles of economic theory; (he) know(s) the basis of social organization and the laws of human psychology" (137). Is this in principle epistemologically possible?

Let us dispense with several more or less foolish objections immediately. The veil of ignorance is a literary device designed to bring to life a logical claim. The claim is simply that in our reasoning about moral and social questions, we can choose to perform the same abstraction from particularities that we have learned to perform in our mathematical reasoning, for example. Just as Rawls does not ask us to believe that there has ever been a person totally without envy, so he does not require us to imagine a creature possessed solely of general knowledge.

Nor is the genetic issue of the sources and development of our knowledge directly relevant, at least not in any trivial way. The general knowledge has no doubt been acquired by induction from, and reflection upon, particulars, including the particulars of the party's own experience; Rawls is in no way denying that obvious truth.

But the parties in the original position *are* rational, and they are therefore presumed to know whatever can be deduced, or otherwise reasonably inferred, from their basic stock of knowledge. They cannot, so to speak, know that all men are animals and that all animals are mortal, and yet forget that all men are mortal.

Now it might be objected that the study of man has yet to yield *laws* of the sort that the natural sciences offer. Such general knowledge as we possess of the basis of social organization or the workings of human psychology is poor stuff compared with the mathematical formulae of physics, chemistry, or even of biology. But though there

121

is undoubtedly much truth in this point, it cannot constitute an objection to Rawls's theory, either in its original version or in the final veil-of-ignorance version. The players in the bargaining game are assumed to be rational, not omniscient. They know whatever intelligent and educated persons can be imagined to know about man and society. If that is a great deal, then their deliberations will be more fruitful; if it is very little, they will have to make do with such estimates as their knowledge warrants. But since, this side of heaven, only subjective rightness can be required of a rational agent, Rawls cannot be faulted merely for the inadequate development of the social sciences.

However, if there are serious methodological or epistemological grounds for supposing that human beings *could not* have the sorts of general knowledge Rawls attributes to the parties in the original position, without their also having to be aware of the sorts of particular facts about themselves that are cloaked by the veil of ignorance—if, in short, the particular combination of knowledge and ignorance required by Rawls's construction is in principle impossible—then the entire theory will be called into question. I do not for a moment suppose that I can prove so strong a claim (though Rawls has said nothing at all to prove its contrary), but I do think there are powerful reasons for at least doubting the cognitive possibility of the original position as Rawls has characterized it.

Consider first the knowledge of political affairs, the principles of economic theory, and the bases of social organization. Rawls's theory assumes that such knowledge is ahistorical in its epistemological foundations, that it has the same trans-temporally impersonal character possessed by the truths of the natural sciences. This is not to say that knowledge of economic theory or social organization is static, that it makes no reference to processes of historical growth or change. The parties in the original position, so far as Rawls is concerned, might know, for example, that the economy of a society must necessarily develop through a determinate series of stages, each defined by the dominant social relationships of production (if, in fact, that *is* a basic fact of society). Or they might know, to make a classical reference, that a just and well-ordered society is prone to degenerate first into a military state, then into an oligarchy, then into a lawless democracy, and finally into a despotic tyranny (cf. Plato's *Republic*). But for Rawls's purposes, it is necessary to suppose that such knowledge, insofar as it *is* knowledge, is timeless, from which it follows that one could at least conceivably possess it no matter where in space or when in time one existed. To be sure, all empirical knowledge is grounded in the previous experience of oneself and others, so a party in the original position who found himself in possession of such knowledge would be able to infer that he was not the first person in the history of the universe. But since the knowledge might (to continue the fantasy) be a legacy from a now-dead civilization, he could not on Rawls's view infer that he was not in the first generation of *his* society, nor could he assume that his own society had experienced whatever was necessary to acquire such knowledge.

But I should like to suggest that Rawls's conception of the nature of knowledge of society is wrong. Following Marx, in the tradition of the discipline usually referred to as the Sociology of Knowledge, I would urge that our knowledge of social reality is fundamentally different from that of natural reality.

Society, or social reality, is a collective human product, in a way that objective nature is not. Society is the sum total of the sentiments, expectations, habits, pat-

123

terns of interactions, and beliefs of the men and women who make it up. The existence and persistence of society requires the systematic hypostatization and objectification of the subjective: the perception by men and women as independently real of social roles and relationships that are in fact dependent upon those who occupy them. Society is thus, as I have elsewhere put it, a sort of *folie à tous.* It is a collective, systematic misperception, or false consciousness, that at one and the same time *expresses* the degree of understanding or misunderstanding of the men and women of a given moment in the history of the society and also *shapes* their feelings, behavior, and expectations so as to sustain or alter that social reality.

The defining mark of collective false consciousness is the belief that society is an *object* governed by immutable laws. These laws, it is thought, can be explored, discovered, formulated, and put to the service of human purposes just as the laws of nature can; but as laws of an objective reality, they cannot be *changed*. They are, it is believed, like the laws of physics. Confronted by an onrushing boulder, one can step out of the way, thereby *avoiding* the consequences of the laws of motion; or one can deflect the boulder by means of a carefully calculated placement of obstacles, thereby *using* the laws of motion; but one cannot, by any amount of meditation, consciousness-raising, or collective self-examination, *abrogate* the laws of motion and so dissolve the threat of the boulder. So too, one can try to avoid the laws of supply and demand, or use the laws of supply and demand, but one cannot abrogate the laws of supply and demand. They are "general facts of human society," and it is a minimal mark of rationality to acknowledge the objectivity of the factual. Or so Rawls's "veil of ignorance" device presupposes.

But the truth, I suggest, is that our knowledge of society is different in kind from our knowledge of nature because the object of our knowledge of society is different in kind from the object of our knowledge of nature. Our knowledge of society is a collective human project, a project of self-understanding *and also of self-alteration.* In order for classical economic theory to develop as a body of knowledge about the operations of the market, it was necessary not merely that a number of extremely smart philosophers make wide-ranging observations and powerful abstractions but also that the patterns of socioeconomic interactions themselves undergo fundamental changes. It was necessary that the cultural, religious, and political dimensions of "economic" activity be separated off, not merely by the observers, the theorists, but also by the participants in those interactions as well. The very forms of personality organization had to change. In short, classical economic theory was not a *discovery* of laws timelessly operative, in the way that Newtonian mechanics was. Rather, it was an expression and reflection of a new form of social organization that had been constituted, brought into existence, by the actions and interactions of countless individuals. The classical economists did not realize this fact, of course. They thought of themselves as *discovering* the laws of the market. The further realization of the real epistemological status of those "laws" was itself a collective social project.

In order for me to "understand" the "discoveries" of classical economics, I must conceive of society in the way that the classical economists did. Otherwise, I would not suppose that they were describing the "real world." And since society, unlike nature, is not an independently existing object—since, indeed, each of us at one and the same time develops a coherent personality by internalizing a social conception of social reality and then sustains (or alters) that social reality by expressing that social conception in social interactions—it follows that I believe an economic theory to be *knowledge* of society only insofar as it expresses the conception of social reality that corresponds to my, and my society's, stage of development in the progressive overcoming of collective false consciousness.

An analogous argument could be made with regard to general knowledge of nature. I cannot be genuinely neutral as between a scientific and an animistic conception of the natural world. I do not mean by this merely that the two conceptions of nature are incompatible, so that a rational man would recognize the necessity of choosing between them. I mean rather that the scientific and animistic orientations toward nature are incompatible ways of knowing and being, so that no one could genuinely engage in a rational deliberation concerning which of them to select. (It is just this sort of point that Kierkegaard makes with such brilliant satirical force in his attacks on the "objective" approach to religious faith.)

Since I have distinguished so sharply between the objects of natural science and the "objects" of social science, it might be supposed that I am denying objective, or scientific, cognitive status to beliefs about society. Not at all. Just as I am sure that the scientific approach to nature is superior to the animistic, so I am confident that scientific history is superior to anecdote, that classical economics was an advance over the medieval theory of the just price, and that the sociology of knowledge is, so far as it has thus far gone, a victory for the human intellect in the battle for knowledge. But whereas natural knowledge is atemporal, social knowledge is historical, self-reflective, and constitutive as well as descriptive.

These remarks, to be sure, are quite general and speculative, but if they have merit, then they call into question Rawls's description of the knowledge-conditions of the original position. I take it as obvious that the parties in the original position are rational, secular, scientific men and women. That fact must be known to them, for it follows from the way they analyze problems of choice and reason about alternatives. Although Rawls makes much of religious toleration and says that it is open in the original position whether the parties have religious beliefs, and if so what they are, that is merely a concession to the liberal tradition of pluralism. If a party in the original position knows that he has a rational plan of life, then he knows that he is not Søren Kierkegaard or Moses or St. Paul, though he may very possibly be Karl Marx or Ramses or Caesar Augustus. By the same token, if the "general facts of human society" include an awareness of the ideological character of classical economic theory, then a party in the original position can infer that he must live in a society that has advanced beyond the stages of hunting and gathering and primitive agriculture, beyond the early stages of the rationalization of industrial production, past even the early stages of the formation of a capitalist economy. He will know that his society has reached or passed a stage at which there is a functional separation and institutionalization of the processes of knowledge acquisition and development, along with a conflict between classes in which the dominant class enlists the services of an intelligentsia to generate a rationalization for what is, but is not yet perceived by all members of the society as, an unjust division of income and wealth. He will know that *his own* society has reached this stage, and not merely that *some* human society in the past has acquired such knowledge, because the knowledge claims advanced by the ideological analysis of economic theory will not appear to him as plausible or comprehensible claims about human society unless his own society has progressed to a certain stage in the progressive demystification of social relationships.

The previous paragraphs are clearly assertions rather than proofs. But they are by no means idiosyncratic or novel assertions. They represent, more or less accurately, one dominant tradition in the social theory of the past century and a half. Rawls's easy assumptions about the knowledge-conditions of the original position merely ignore the arguments and analyses of this tradition in favor of an older, and I believe less subtle and defensible tradition. At the very least, I suggest, one cannot accept the veil of ignorance and the original position as plausible analytic constructions, for the purpose of explicating and defending a theory of justice, until one has settled this epistemological dispute concerning the nature of our knowledge of society.

An analogous problem is posed by the concept of a well-ordered society, which we have already looked at briefly. The distinctive mark of a well-ordered society is *publicity*—"everyone accepts and knows that the others accept the same principles of justice" (5). Rawls states that he intends to limit his discussion to "the principles of justice that would regulate a well-ordered society" (8). He describes this as a decision to deal with "strict compliance as opposed to partial compliance theory," which seems to imply that the difference between a well-ordered and a non-well-ordered society lies in the degree to which individuals know, abide by, and know that others abide by, the principles of justice. In subsequent chapters, Rawls treats it as an open question whether a society governed in a well-ordered manner by his two principles of justice will have a socialist or a capitalist economy. But suppose that Marx is correct about the relationship between systematic class-exploitation and the existence of false consciousness and ideology in a society (as I suspect in some sense he is). Suppose that the private ownership and control of the means of production, and production for profit rather than for need, are socially insupportable without widespread, systematic misconceptions about the real nature of economic, power, and political relationships. Then it would in principle be impossible for a well-ordered society to have a capitalist economic structure, for by the time the publicity conditions required by the concept of well-ordering had been achieved—indeed, before they had been fully achieved—a revolutionary change in the social relationships of production would have taken place.

Once again, I hasten to acknowledge that I have merely suggested a possibility rather than argued, let alone proved, a case. But even this suggestion, backed as it is by a century of impressive social theory, suffices to show that Rawls has packed extremely powerful, and I venture to say ideologically biased, assumptions into his characterization of the original position under the veil of ignorance.

When we turn to Rawls's assertion that the parties in the original position know the "laws of human psychology," we encounter analogous methodological and epistemological problems. [35] Here, too, the difficulty lies in Rawls's easy assumption that knowledge of human personality, like knowledge of bodies in motion, is atemporal and impersonal. I realize that some such assumption is widely shared by many schools of social psychology and personality theory, but I suggest that it is quite emphatically *not* shared by Freud and those who have followed him in the psychoanalytic tradition. In appealing to Freud's methods and insights, I am once again in the position merely of expressing my intellectual

[35] The following several pages owe whatever coherence and cogency they may possess to the help of my wife, Professor Cynthia Griffin Wolff.

commitments and preferences. I must ask the reader to consider these remarks for what they are, and to consult his own convictions in these matters.

The key to Freud's work, I take it, is his discovery of the unconscious. Simplifying considerably, we may say that our minds are always working at two levels, the conscious and the unconscious. Each of us apprehends and responds to cues, or messages from others at both levels; and each of us communicates with others consciously and unconsciously. Through the dynamic processes of projection, transference, displacement, and repression, and through the deployment of elaborately self-deceptive defenses, we transform, hide, or deny painful, or shameful, or dangerous desires, thoughts, and feelings. No account of human experience and behavior could be adequate without the acknowledgment of this rich complexity of the conscious and the unconscious.

Now, the psychoanalyst in treating a patient responds to him emotionally—responds as a human being—in addition to observing him clinically. The psychoanalyst uses his spontaneous emotional responses as clues to the latent communications from the patient's unconscious. If the psychoanalyst denies or represses his own emotional responses in the interest of scientific objectivity or clinical impersonality, he deprives himself of an indispensable tool of investigation and interpretation.

Even more significantly, however, as later psychoanalysts came to realize, a process of "counter-transference" takes place in the therapeutic situation. Not only does the patient, in a successful therapy, transfer his fantasies to the analyst, but the analyst himself experiences a reciprocal transference of his own fantasies (which he, as a human being, must also harbor in his unconscious). Here, again, the way to insight and understanding lies not through suppression but rather through self-reflective acceptance by the analyst of these processes in himself.

Thus far, one might suppose that Rawls could easily accept everything I have said, assuming that he is as impressed as I am with the insights and methods of psychoanalysis. For it is only as participants in the original position that the parties are ignorant of their particular personalities and life histories. It is perfectly consistent with Rawls's theory to assert that their acquisition of a knowledge of the "laws of human psychology" has involved them personally and directly in self-reflective interactions with other human beings. But to argue in this way would be to assume that once an individual has arrived at an understanding of a particular person, or of emotional pathology in general, he can bracket his self-knowledge in order to leave standing a body of objective, impersonal scientific knowledge. I suggest, to the contrary, that knowledge arrived at through a recognition, acceptance, and transcendence of one's own projections and transferences carries with it the mark of its origins. A young analyst's understanding of an old patient's fantasies, defenses, and emotions will necessarily differ from the understanding—quite possibly equally therapeutically successful—of an elderly analyst. A male analyst will have a different understanding of the emotional significance of pregnancy and birth from a female analyst. And—though age and sex are different in kind from color as differentiators of human beings—in our society a black analyst will have a different understanding of the emotional significance of race from a white analyst.

I am not asserting that only the old can understand the old, only men can understand men, only women women, only whites whites, and only blacks blacks. Rather, I am saying that each of us understands others, either informally in our day-to-day contacts, or clinically as trained therapists, through the mediation of our own fundamental emotional composition. Hence, our knowledge bears the mark of the knower as well as the mark of the known. To assert that the parties in the original position will know the laws of human psychology without knowing who they are, and whether they are old or young, male or female, white or black, homosexual or heterosexual, is to say that they will actually *understand* the laws of human psychology, not merely that they will mouth certain empty phrases. And that, I suggest, is not possible, if Freud and the psychoanalytic tradition is correct.

These remarks about the "general facts of human society" constitute an extended complaint that Rawls has neglected Marx and Freud. Libraries have been written about each of these figures and the intellectual traditions they began. My own intellectual commitment, obviously, is to those traditions, and I hope that readers who share my inclinations will agree that Rawls has failed to do them justice. But to those other readers who doubt or reject the orientations of Marx or Freud, I would suggest that there is something suspect about a theoretical construction, designed to capture the essential features of deliberative rationality, which rules out Freud and Marx *ab initio*.

XIV

Primary Goods and Life-Plans[36]

I N addition to their knowledge of the general facts of
human society and the particular fact that their society exhibits the circumstances of justice, the parties in
the original position are said to know that as rational
human beings they have coherent, integrated plans of
life. Furthermore, although they do not know the details
of those plans, they do know that the plans require certain sorts of goods for their satisfactory completion.
These "primary goods" are such that each party, in ignorance of the details of his plan of life, knows that he
prefers more of them rather than less. As we have seen,
these assumptions, abstract though they may appear,
carry a good deal of substantive weight—or, perhaps
more accurately, place extremely narrow substantive
constraints on the choice problem confronting the parties in the original position.

In the first formulation of the theory of primary goods,
Rawls identifies them as falling into the general
categories of "rights and liberties, opportunities and
powers, income and wealth" (92). Subsequently, he revises this account to give priority to rights and liberties,
and he somewhat alters both the wording and the interpretation of the two principles to give expression to
this ordering. I have already dealt with the priority of
liberty in Part Two. At this point, therefore, let us focus
our attention on the notion of a plan of life and its re-

[36] With this section, see especially Michael Teitelman, "The
Limits of Individualism," *J. Phil.*, 69 (1972), and Rawls's reply to that
and other criticisms in "Fairness to Goodness," *Phil. Review* (1975),
pp. 536–54.

quirement of "opportunities and powers, income and wealth."

First of all, I propose to set aside any objections to Rawls's theory based on the possibility of ascetic or quasi-religious plans of life. To be sure, if a man has taken as his motto Thoreau's injunction to "Simplify, simplify" then beyond a very modest level he will not have positive marginal utility for primary goods (leaving aside rights and liberties, and "a sense of one's own worth"). But if the worst that can be said of justice as fairness is that it misses the peculiar appeal of asceticism, then Rawls will have very little to worry about. Besides, ascetics ought not to concern themselves with consideration of distributive justice, particularly if they are not envious.

But although it is acceptable to assume that every rational man will want more of any primary good rather than less, it is not so clear that rational men of differing life-plan persuasions will exhibit even a rough agreement on the proper way to rank or order differing bundles of disparate primary goods. Rawls for the most part finesses this problem by referring to "an index of primary goods." However, save for the not very useful unanimity quasi-ordering rule, there are no obvious ways of establishing such an index. "Income and wealth" seem easy enough, since in a market economy the price system will serve as an indexing mechanism, but how are we to factor in "opportunities and powers?"[37] This is by no means a trivial matter, as we can see by imagining how differing life-plans would call forth incompatible weightings or indexings of primary goods.

[37] For some illuminating remarks on the indexing problem, as well as an important discussion of the maximin rule, see Kenneth Arrow, "Some Ordinalist-Utilitarian Notes on Rawls' Theory of Justice," in *J. Phil.*, 70 (1973), pp. 245–63.

Compare two hypothetical "representative men." The first seeks to maximize his acquisition and enjoyment of consumer goods, even at the price of a certain artificiality and standardization of life experiences. He is prepared to accept rather strict labor discipline on the job, to work long hours, and to adjust his consumption patterns to the ever-changing array of goods offered for sale. The second values flexibility and independence on the job, and a more "natural" style of consumption, based on a relatively limited, but stable, market of familiar goods. Both individuals have rational plans of life, but their indexing of bundles of opportunities and powers, wealth and income, will diverge widely.

If a society contains two very large groups of persons whose plans of life exhibit roughly the characteristic shapes of the plans sketched here, their different indexing of primary goods will be translated into competing, and quite possibly incompatible, social policies. Merely choosing to maximize the index of primary goods of the least advantaged representative person in the society will not *solve* the indexing problem. Quite to the contrary, it will *pose* it in a way that a rule of maximizing income and wealth alone will not. Rawls, on occasion, seeks to avoid this problem, which he very well understands, by suggesting that the distribution of nonmonetary primary goods tends to vary directly with that of income and wealth. But he offers no evidence for this claim, and it does seem to me that there is a limit to the number of ad hoc assumptions one can incorporate into a formal model designed to generate a significant theorem.[38]

Here, as in so many other places, we see Rawls's original conception of the choice problem operating beneath the surface of his much more elaborate final theory. In

[38] See Barber, "Justifying Justice," p. 303.

135

its simplest (and most elegant) form, the choice problem was a problem of pure income distribution. The good being distributed was measurable, divisible, transferable, and hence manageable by the formal model of a bargaining game. But in response to criticisms, difficulties, and implausibilities, Rawls enriches his portrait of the choice problem until it becomes thoroughly unmanageable. It is difficult enough for a single individual with a rational plan of life to index a heterogeneous bundle of primary goods so as to compare it with other bundles, especially if he is not permitted to take the easy way out by merely "expressing" an unreasoned and inexplicable "preference." But to define, even in the roughest way, an indexing procedure that is to be neutral as among alternative plans of life is, I suggest, simply impossible. Any attempt must inevitably make some substantive appeal to one sort of life-plan (or perhaps, one class of sorts of life-plans) and hence build normative or cultural biases into what is intended as a value-neutral procedure.

As I have remarked, Rawls's conception of a rational plan of life is in a long and honorable philosophical tradition. His summary statement of the conception is as clear as one could ask:

> The main idea is that a person's good is determined by what is for him the most rational long-term plan of life given reasonably favorable circumstances. A man is happy when he is more or less successfully in the way of carrying out this plan. To put it briefly, the good is the satisfaction of rational desire. We are to suppose, then, that each individual has a rational plan of life drawn up subject to the conditions that confront him. This plan is designed to permit the harmonious satisfaction of his interests. It schedules activities so that various desires can be fulfilled without interference. It is arrived at by re-

jecting other plans that are either less likely to succeed or do not provide for such an inclusive attainment of aims. Given the alternatives available, a rational plan is one which cannot be improved upon; there is no other plan which, taking everything into account, would be preferable. [92–93].

There are two difficulties with this notion of a plan of life, both of which seem to me to detract from the plausibility and universal acceptability of Rawls's theory. The first is that the conception is excessively culture-bound, so that it builds into the supposedly formal constraints of the original position certain unexpressed assumptions that give ideological expression to a particular socio-economic configuration and set of interests; the second is that, as Rawls conceives it, the ideal of a rational plan of life conflicts with the organic, developmental character of a healthy human personality.

Consider first the sort of human society in which it would be materially possible to formulate and live out something answering to Rawls's description of a rational plan of life. The society would have to be extremely stable—not in its possession and recognition of a conception of justice, but simply in the continuity and predictability of career lines, marriage practices, child-rearing arrangements, and so forth. In a rapidly changing society or one whose future was materially unsettled, plans of life would collapse into contingency plans or even into rules of thumb about holding oneself at the ready for whatever might come.

Even within a settled and stable society, the sort of plan of life Rawls describes is more characteristic of the professional middle classes than of working-class men and women. In modern America, for example, doctors tend to remain doctors throughout their working lives, and professors tend to remain professors; but the aver-

137

age worker can expect to hold jobs falling into many entirely different categories in the course of a working life. Now Rawls knows this, of course, and his discussion is punctuated by qualifications, caveats, and acknowledgments of the uncertainty of human existence. Faced with the facts of average job change, for example, a young American might conclude that a general liberal education, suited to the demands of flexibility and repeated "retooling," would be, "taking everything into account," the most rational first stage of a plan of life.

But there comes a point at which qualifications dissolve the coherence of a conception. If we stand back a bit from the fretwork of Rawls's sometimes overly protective language and attempt to form an image of the sort of person who would fit his descriptions, there comes into view quite clearly a professional man (the book is rather heavily laden with male-oriented language), launched upon a career, living in a stable political, social, and economic environment, in which reasoned decisions can be made about such long-term matters as life insurance, residential location, schooling for the children, and retirement. The temporal orientation is essentially toward the future rather than toward the past, but toward the future as a whole, not toward some particular dramatic or ecstatic moment in the future. In short, what we see is exactly what Karl Mannheim characterized, in his brilliant discussion of the ideological structure of time-consciousness, as the liberal-humanitarian utopian mentality.[39]

The second problem is that, like all ideologies, this conception of rational plans of life is a *misrepresentation* of the reality of human experience, not a correct representation of one special style of human experience.

[39] Karl Mannheim, *Ideology and Utopia*, Part IV.

Hence, over and above the fact that it is special rather than general, it is also distorted rather than accurate. The model of rationality being invoked here by Rawls is a model appropriate to a firm rather than to an individual human being. In a sense, Rawls adapts to his own uses a mode of argument deployed by Plato in the *Gorgias*. Plato begins with the ordinary notion of a *techné*, or "art," and the condition, or "virtue," of the "artist" in virtue of which he can perform well his proper function as an artist. He then asks what the proper function or *techné* of the soul is, concludes that it is "to live," and infers that there must be some healthy condition of the soul, some virtue, that enables it to live well—that is, to perform its proper function appropriately. So too, Rawls begins with the notion of prudential rationality appropriate to economic activity, and with the associated notion that a rational firm will have a long-run plan of profit maximization, rather than merely a settled tendency to seize whatever profit-making opportunities present themselves each day. Employing as his analysis of individual rationality those formal models that have been developed in the theory of economic activity, Rawls treats the living of a life as analogous to the directing of a firm. A rationally lived life will be guided by a long-range plan, and a life, like a firm, will be doing well when the plan is "more or less successfully in the way" of being carried out.

There are, of course, problems with the economic notion of a rational plan of profit-maximization, one of the knottiest of which is the question of the length of time over which results are to be summed in calculating the returns. It is not surprising, in light of these observations, that Rawls treats the relationship between fathers and sons as somehow inextricably bound up with an appropriate choice of a social rate of savings.

But the living of a life is not at all like the managing of a firm. A firm is a legal person, but not an organic, natural, living creature. A human being has an infancy, a childhood, an adolescence, a young adulthood, a mature adulthood, and an old age. What is "rational" at one stage in the life cycle is irrational, unhealthy, at another. It is fitting that a young man or woman should dream dreams of great achievement, of limitless futures, of time without end. In a man or woman of mature years, the very same dreams are a flight from reality, a truth-denying fantasy. An adolescent who formulates a life-plan, complete with sinking funds, contingency allowances, and a persistent concern for a solid pension plan, will almost certainly miss much of the joy and satisfaction that life holds out for us. When I read that Immanuel Kant twice took so long to calculate the benefits and burdens of marriage that the object of his possible affections made other marital arrangements, I do not judge that he was rationally pursuing a prudent life-plan; I conclude that he was not the marrying kind, and that he was obviously better off a bachelor.

Michael Oakeshott, the distinguished English conservative political philosopher, has perfectly captured the bizarre notion of "reason" underlying the notion of a rational plan of life in his coruscating essay, "Rationalism in Politics." The following lines say, better than I am able, what is wrong with Rawls's conception:

[T]he mind of the Rationalist . . . impresses us as, at best, a finely-tempered, neutral instrument, as a well-trained rather than as an educated mind. Intellectually, his ambition is not so much to share the experience of the race as to be demonstrably a self-made man. And this gives to his intellectual and practical activities an almost preternatural deliberateness and self-consciousness, depriving them of any element of passivity, removing from them all sense of rhythm and continuity and dissolving them into a succession of climacterics, each to be surmounted by a *tour de raison*. His mind has no atmosphere, no changes of season and temperature; his intellectual processes, so far as possible, are insulated from all external influence and go on in a void. . . . With an almost poetic fancy, he strives to live each day as if it were his first, and he believes that to form a habit is to fail.[40]

I can think of no more perfect characterization of the parties in the original position, nor of a less persuasive portrait of true *rationality*.

[40] Michael Oakeshott, *Rationalism in Politics* (Basic Books, 1962), pp. 2–3.

XV

A Formal Analysis of the Bargaining Game

ONCE again, it will prove useful to creep up on the problem by stages. First we shall analyze the game described by Rawls in the first version of his theory, as set forth in "Justice as Fairness." Then we shall briefly take account of a qualification, added by Rawls in that essay, that alters the game but does not significantly alter our analysis. Third, we shall lower the veil of ignorance and reconstruct the game accordingly, leaving to one side, however, the special problems raised by the fact that the players under the veil do not know where in time or space they are. Once we are clear about that form of the game, we will complicate things to take account of this last bit of original-position ignorance, and then see what we have come up with in the way of a bargaining game.

With the structure of the game clarified, we can then confront Rawls's complex and controversial use of the maximin rule of choice under uncertainty. I shall offer a few slightly technical remarks on the subject, drawn in part from Luce and Raiffa, John Harsanyi, and others, intended to call that use into question. Finally, by way of conclusion, I shall say a bit about the notion of pure procedural justice.

STRUCTURE OF THE GAME

The Game in "Justice as Fairness"

I shall assume, for the sake of simplicity, that Rawls's bargaining game is to be construed as a non-cooperative

142

game, in which there is no preplay communication.[41]
Each player is thus permitted just one move, which consists of writing his proposal for the principles of justice
on a piece of paper and handing it to the referee. In
order to make standard game theory relevant, we shall
suppose that there are only finitely many different principles that can be proposed and that each player is
handed a list of them, n in all. Each player then has just
$n + 1$ strategies: he can write down any of the n principles on the list, or he can leave his paper blank. The last
alternative is equivalent to opting for the state of nature
that prevailed before the game began.[42]

Assuming that there are only finitely many players,
say m, it follows that there are $(n + 1)^m$ different combinations of strategies that may be handed to the referee,
and each of these will, by the rules of the game, be associated with an outcome. In the simplest case, where
there is only one possible principle of justice and two
players, each of the players will have two strategies (to
propose that principle or to leave his paper blank), and
there will be four outcomes—thus giving us the familiar
two-by-two outcome matrix so often seen in game theory
texts. Since the rules of the game say that a principle will
be adopted if and only if it is chosen unanimously, the
outcome matrix of this simple game will look like Figure
1.

[41] The reasons for this assumption are spelled out in the Technical
Appendix to Section V.

[42] In this version of the game, there are exactly as many strategies
for each player as there are principles plus leaving the paper blank.
In any form of the cooperative version, even one allowing for only a
single go round the circle, the number of *strategies* balloons as-
tronomically. For a formal definition of a strategy, see Luce and
Raiffa, *Games and Decisions*, pp. 51–52. I shall not try to take account of the possibility of mixed strategies, which really does mess
things up horribly.

Player 2

		Principle 1	Leave Paper Blank
Player 1	Principle 1	Principle 1 is adopted	State of Nature
	Leave Paper Blank	State of Nature	State of Nature

FIGURE 1

When there are two players and more available principles, the matrix will still be two-dimensional, but it will be bigger. With four principles, we get a five-by-five outcome matrix looking like Figure 2. For m players, we

Player 2

		Princ. 1	Princ. 2	Princ. 3	Princ. 4	Blank
Player 1	Princ. 1	Princ. 1 adopted	State of Nature	State of Nature	State of Nature	State of Nature
	Princ. 2	State of Nature	Princ. 2 adopted	State of Nature	State of Nature	State of Nature
	Princ. 3	State of Nature	State of Nature	Princ. 3 adopted	State of Nature	State of Nature
	Princ. 4	State of Nature	State of Nature	State of Nature	Princ. 4 adopted	State of Nature
	Blank	State of Nature	State of Nature	State of Nature	State of Nature	State of Nature

FIGURE 2

will require an m-dimensional array, each edge of which will be $n + 1$ terms in length. All the entries in the array will read "State of Nature" except for those that correspond to unanimous coordination on one or another of the n available principles. There are thus $n + 1$ distinct outcomes, and a little geometric imagination will reveal that they form a diagonal of the m-dimensional array running, so to speak, from northwest to southeast.

The next step is for each player to calculate the value to himself of each possible outcome, so that we can construct a "payoff matrix." The payoff matrix has the same structure as the outcome matrix, but where the outcome matrix lists an outcome ("Principle 1 adopted," "Principle 9 adopted," "State of Nature," and so forth), the payoff matrix will list an ordered m-tuple of numbers representing the value to each of the m players of that outcome.

To begin with, each player presumably knows what value he places on the state of nature in which he found himself before entering the bargaining game, so he fills in that value wherever appropriate. Each player also knows each other player's evaluations, and no one is allowed to misrepresent his preferences (these are all wildly implausible, standard game theoretic assumptions). But things get more difficult when it comes to filling the values for the non-state-of-nature outcomes. What each player must do is to perform an extremely complicated calculation of expected utility, in which he estimates the system of practices with associated distribution that is likely to come about in his society if it is governed by the principle under consideration; estimates the probabilities that he will fill the various representative positions in that system; calculates the value to him of occupying those positions, suitably discounted

145

by their probabilities; and finally, given such uncertainties of life as unemployment, industrial injuries, etc., makes one grand summation of all the possible outcomes multiplied by their values and discounted by their probabilities. That number he plugs into his slot in the appropriate m-tuple. He does this for each principle, and once again we assume that he knows, or is told, the value that each player puts into each slot. After each player has made his calculations and everyone has a correct, fully-filled-in payoff matrix next to the list of available principles and his ballot, we are ready to play the game. [43]

At this point, Rawls proposes that each player choose a strategy by means of the maximin rule. This rule is usually explained in connection with two-person games that can be represented graphically by a two-dimensional array of rows and columns. One can then talk about the "minimum entry in a row" or the "maximum entry in a column," and so forth. In an m-person game, however, the payoffs are represented by an m-dimensional array, and the outcomes corresponding to a particular strategy choice by one player consist of an $(m - 1)$-dimensional array, not of a row or column. (A row, of course, is simply a one-dimensional array, which is to say a $[2 - 1]$-dimensional array.) At the risk of compounding confusion, I shall speak in what follows of multidimensional arrays, not of rows or columns. The graphic examples, however, will all be in the form of familiar two-dimensional matrices.

At any rate, a player first examines the $(m - 1)$-dimensional array that represents all of the different

---

[43] Nothing has been said about the interpersonal comparability of the numbers in the payoff matrix, but in view of the process by which they are derived, it *is* clear that they are cardinally significant. These issues do not play a role in our discussion, however, until later in this section.

payoffs he might get as a result of adopting a particular strategy (depending on what the other players do), and he locates the smallest payoff in the array. This is his "security level." Were he to choose that strategy, that is the worst that could happen to him. He then looks at the security level of each strategy available to him and selects the strategy with the highest security level—the strategy with the maximum minimum payoff. In performing this calculation, he ignores all the other payoffs, regardless of their magnitude and distribution. He also makes no attempt to estimate the likelihood of other players' choices. If there are several strategies with the same maximum security level, and if none of them can be eliminated from consideration by virtue of what is known as "weak domination,"[44] then the entire set of strategies with the maximum security level is considered the "correct" choice for the player, and he simply selects one at random.

In the particular game we are considering, a player's payoff will be the same for every entry in a given array, j (namely, the value he places on the state of nature), save for the entry corresponding to the outcome, "Principle j adopted." There are three possibilities: the adoption of principle j may, by the player's calculation, be worth to him more than the state of nature, less than the state of nature, or the same amount as the state of nature. If the adoption of principle j is worth more to him than the state of nature, then his security level for that array will be his state of nature value. If principle j is worth the

---

[44] One strategy "weakly dominates" another if the first pays at least as well as the second no matter what the other players choose, and actually pays better for at least one of the choices of the other players. Obviously if a player has two such strategies available to him, he will never choose the second, since the first *must* do at least as well for him and *may* do better.

same to him as the state of nature, the state of nature value will be his security level. But if principle j is worth less to him than the state of nature, then that smaller value will be his security level.

Now consider: one array, that corresponding to the state of nature option, must have the state of nature value as its security level. What is more, no array can have more than the state of nature value as its security level, inasmuch as every array has many state of nature entries. Therefore, the maximum security level of the matrix, for each player, is the state of nature level. There is just one, and only one, set of circumstances under which a rational player, choosing his strategy by the maximin rule, can be counted on to select the difference principle as his strategy. If *every other principle* offers the player a lower payoff, if adopted, than the state of nature, and the difference principle offers him more than the state of nature, then he will choose the difference principle. Security level considerations will eliminate all strategies save the difference principle and the state of nature option, and weak dominance considerations will eliminate the state of nature option. But if there are as many as *two* principles (taking into account transfer payments and compensations) that, if adopted, offer him more than the state of nature, then maximin will instruct him to randomize over the set of such principles, and with m players randomizing in this way, the probability of coordination will be extremely small.

There is no way of judging, in general, whether there will be any, or many, principles whose adoption offers a given player more than what he can get from a state of nature, but I think it is fair to say that Rawls thinks there will be at least several, and, if that is the case, then his theorem is invalid.

The Game in "Justice as Fairness" with Pessimism Added

Thus far, we have been analyzing the first form of Rawls's model on the assumption that players fill in the payoff matrix by carrying out expected utility calculations. But in "Justice as Fairness," Rawls seems to suggest that they proceed in a different, and much more pessimistic, manner. The principles proposed by the players "will express the conditions in accordance with which each is the least unwilling to have his interests limited in the design of practices, given the competing interests of the other, on the supposition that the interests of others will be limited likewise. The restrictions which would so arise might be thought of as those a person would keep in mind if he were designing a practice in which his enemy were to assign him his place" (138–39).

The language, in particular the phrase "least unwilling," suggests that Rawls conceives this proposal as a form of maximin, but in fact it is a proposal for constructing the payoff matrix from the outcome matrix, not a proposal for choosing a strategy once the payoff matrix has been completed. Since no assumptions have been made about the various players' utility functions, this new constraint will not suffice to make the payoff matrix symmetric.[45] It will, for some players, reduce the size of the set of strategies over which they randomize (roughly, it reduces the set, for a player whose natural talents, or whatever, give him promising results from the various expected utility calculations carried out to construct the payoff matrix); but the shape of the problem remains unchanged. Not even a double application of maximin, first

[45] That is, the m-tuples will not, in general, be strings of identical numbers.

149

in the construction of the payoff matrix and then in the choice of strategy, will produce the "solution" Rawls seeks.

The Game under the Veil of Ignorance: First Approximation

When the veil of ignorance is lowered, the game changes in a number of extremely important ways. Players no longer know who they are, where in historical time or space they or their societies are located, what their utility functions are, or even how many players there are at any one moment in real time. Under the circumstances it becomes, to put it mildly, a trifle difficult to construct a payoff matrix. There is, however, one compensating gain, which Rawls makes much of: leaving aside such sophistications as chance or random elements in the determination of payoff values, the players' ignorance destroys any grounds on which they could assign different values to a given outcome. As a consequence, the payoff matrix, when it is constructed, should be *symmetric*.

The players as yet have no idea what they want, and hence no way of knowing how well or badly various states of affairs will satisfy them. Rawls therefore assumes that all players have a "plan of life"; that some identifiable subset of the distributable things in a society is especially helpful in pursuing any rational plan of life one might adopt, and hence can be called "primary goods"; that no other distributable things are terribly important to any rational plan of life, so that a player's utility will depend solely on what he gets of those primary goods; and, of course, that all players want more primary goods rather than less, so that they have positive marginal utility (over some realistic interval) for a suitable index of primary goods. The ignorance conditions also require, as a highly significant simplification, that all players be imagined to have identically the same utility function.

The first problem in the construction of the payoff matrix is the selection of a value for the state of nature outcomes. Even though the players are assumed to live, prior to the bargain, under the "conditions of justice," one of which is a rough equality in power, we must assume that there is a very significant difference between the condition of the worst-off and best-off representative individuals in the state of nature. The tenor of Rawls's reasoning makes it clear that there are only two possible values for the state of nature entries: either that of the worst-off individual in the state of nature or that of the best-off.[46] At this point, we are assuming, provisionally, that the players know *what* society they live in, but not *who* in the society they are. States of nature, we must recall, are not loin-cloth jungle romps, or wars of all against all, but simply social situations in which no principles of justice have been agreed upon.

Now, the idea underlying Rawls's argument is that players in the bargaining game must be cautious, conservative, even pessimistic in their calculations. They must not rush headlong into an agreement they will later regret. If a player assumes that he is one of the worst-off persons in his state of nature, then he will be excessively eager to conclude a bargain, for any principle whose adoption promises the worst-off person more than what the worst-off gets in the state of nature will be attractive to him. When he regains full knowledge of himself, he

[46] Some kind of averaging might seem attractive as a compromise, but once Rawls permits his players to engage in averaging in order to arrive at a value for the state of nature, he will be hard put to deny them the same device in evaluating the payoffs for the various principles, and that way lies utilitarianism and heaven knows what else.

151

may find that he was *not* one of the worst off in the state of nature, and that his agreement has actually lowered his payoff. So *pessimism* tells him to assume that he is best off in the state of nature. The same pessimism, of course, also tells him to assume that he will be worst off under the operation of the principles agreed upon. So it would appear that the following simple set of rules captures Rawls's conception of the rational way to construct the payoff matrix:

1. To each state of nature outcome, assign the value of that state of nature to the best-off representative individual in it.

2. To each adoption-of-a-principle outcome, assign the value of the adoption of that principle to the worst-off representative individual under it.

There is only one problem with this proposal. If we assume, as seems reasonable, that the *worst-off* representative individual under any of the proposed principles will not be as well off as the *best-off* representative individual in the state of nature (there are, after all, limits to the potentialities of social cooperation), then the state-of-nature option will weakly dominate every other strategy, and the outcome of the game will be a return to the state of nature!

If players make the *optimistic* assumption that they are the worst-off individuals in the state of nature, and couple that with the pessimistic assumption that they will be worst off under any of the principles, then we do get a payoff matrix of some interest. The maximin rule of choice still will not permit us to reach a determinate solution, for all of the reasons analyzed above, but with a number of further complications and assumptions, we might actually arrive at Rawls's difference principle. The matrices in Figures 3, 4, and 5, for two players and two

Player 2

	Principle 1	Principle 2	Blank
Principle 1	11, 17	10, 15	10, 15
Principle 2	10, 15	18, 13	10, 15
Blank	10, 15	10, 15	10, 15

Player 1 (row label)

FIGURE 3. THE "TRUE" MATRIX

Player 2

	Principle 1	Principle 2	Blank
Principle 1	11, 11	15, 15	15, 15
Principle 2	15, 15	13, 13	15, 15
Blank	15, 15	15, 15	15, 15

Player 1 (row label)

FIGURE 4. THE "PESSIMISTIC" MATRIX

Player 2

	Principle 1	Principle 2	Blank
Principle 1	11, 11	10, 10	10, 10
Principle 2	10, 10	13, 13	10, 10
Blank	10, 10	10, 10	10, 10

Player 1 (row label)

FIGURE 5. THE "OPTIMISTIC" MATRIX

153

principles plus the state of nature, should make the situation clear. The numbers, as usual, are for illustration only.

Figure 3 shows the true values, for players 1 and 2, of the state of nature and the adoption of principles 1 and 2 (leaving to one side all questions of interpersonal comparisons of utility, etc.). Figure 4 is the payoff matrix that would be constructed by adopting a pessimistic view of the bargaining process: each player assumes that he is best off in the state of nature and will be worst off under any principle adopted. Quite clearly each player's third strategy (leave blank) weakly dominates the other two, and the outcome will be a reversion to the state of nature. Figure 5 is the payoff matrix constructed by combining optimism about the bargaining process in general (i.e., that one has a great deal to gain by the process) with pessimism about the outcome of the process (that one will be worst off under any set of principles adopted). There aren't any very good reasons for taking this point of view, but it does yield a manageable game. Strategies 1 and 2 weakly dominate strategy 3 for each player, and so the game reduces to a two-by-two game. Maximin will still give both strategies as the solution set. But symmetry encourages us to believe that players will cooperate on principle 2 if they are allowed to communicate, or coordinate on principle 2 if they are not.

May we then conclude, at long last, that we have hit upon a way of construing the game that yields the difference principle as its solution? Since the difference principle, by definition, maximizes the payoff to the worst-off representative individual (and then, lexically to each less badly off representative individual), the entry for the adoption of the difference principle, given symmetry, will surely be the outcome either of cooperation or coordination.

154

Not quite. Rawls must make one more assumption before he can adopt the analysis presented here (or his own analysis, for that matter) and declare the difference principle the solution to the game. The assumption may seem trivial, and mentioning it may seem pointlessly obstructive, but for reasons that I shall try to explain in Part Five, I believe that the ease with which Rawls makes the assumption tells us a great deal about what is wrong with his approach to the subject of social philosophy.

Briefly, we must assume that when a principle is adopted, it is certain that the society that has adopted it will come, in time, to instantiate it. He has slipped this extraordinarily powerful assumption into his argument in the very opening pages by his definition of a "well-ordered society" as a society in which "(1) everyone accepts and knows that the others accept the same principles of justice, and (2) *the basic social institutions generally satisfy* and are generally known to satisfy these principles" (p. 5, emphasis added).

Rawls is free to limit himself to a consideration of well-ordered societies, as I have already noted, but he is *not* free to assume without argument that any particular principle, such as the difference principle, can in fact *be* the principle of a well-ordered society. A knowledge of the basic facts of society might reveal that, when a society self-consciously adopts the difference principle, it fails, despite its best efforts, to maximize the index of primary goods assigned to the worst-off representative individual. Economists and sociologists from Adam Smith to the present have warned us of the unexpected consequences of the most publicly spirited, morally admirable social policies. Raise the minimum wage, Milton Friedman claims, and you increase unemployment by driving capitalists to substitute labor-saving techniques that were unprofitable at the lower wage. Clamp down on the flow of heroin into the country and you touch off a crime wave as the soaring street price pushes addicts into ever-more violent thefts. By brushing aside such considerations, Rawls simply denies the social nature of society.

The Game under the Veil of Ignorance: Second Approximation

In the official version of the original position, the players do not even know what actual society they come from. They have no idea what its level of technology is, or what stage of socio-political development it has reached. But they do know the truth of a vast number of conditional propositions that can be imagined as having the form: "If we are in society and economy of type t, then the adoption of principle j will, assuming that the society is well-ordered, lead to a pattern and level of distribution of primary goods, d, in which the population will be divided into income categories, or social classes, or representative individuals x, y, z, etc." (I have already indicated why I think it would be impossible for the players to possess only information of this general sort.) It follows that there will not be one state of nature for the players to fall back on in the absence of agreement, but as many different states of nature as there are different possible social realities. And to each principle on the list of available principles of justice there will be associated not *one* outcome in the event of its adoption, but a range of outcomes, one for each different social reality in which it might be put into operation.

The most natural way to represent this additional complication is to construct an $m + 1$ dimensional outcome matrix in which "reality" is treated as the $m + 1$st

156

player.[47] We can imagine that while each player is selecting a strategy from among the n principles and the state of nature option, "reality" is independently selecting an actual socio-economic state of affairs in which the principle will be put into operation. The players know what options reality has, and they know what the result will be of combining any one of those options with one of the available principles (this is what it means, I take it, to know the basic facts of society, etc.). Hence they will be able to construct the outcome matrix.

In constructing the payoff matrix, the players are apparently to be extremely optimistic about the bargaining game as such—which means that they are to assign to each possible state of nature outcome the value of that outcome to the worst-off individual under it. Now, however, since we have a dimension of the matrix along which social reality varies, there will be as many different such values as there are different possible social realities.

Rawls claims that it is rational for the players to be utterly pessimistic (or cautious) in evaluating the outcomes corresponding to the adoption of the various principles in the various possible social realities. This means assigning to each such outcome the value of that social reality, as organized by the principle in question, to the worst-off representative individual. We shall have to examine Rawls's reasons for proposing so pessimistic a rule for constructing the payoff matrix.

---

[47] In standard discussions of decision problems under uncertainty, the extra player is referred to as "nature," and games of this sort are called "games against nature." In this case, however, it is not the nature of nature, but the nature of society that is in question, and so "reality" is a better term. Cf. Luce and Raiffa, *Games and Decisions*, Chapter 13, where the case of *individual* choice under uncertainty is discussed at length.

Finally, with the payoff matrix set, Rawls asserts that the rational rule of choice is maximin. (Since the payoff matrix, under the veil of ignorance, is symmetric, the choice problem is of course the same for each player.) Now, however, maximin carries a new, and doubly pessimistic, signification. As a player considers each strategy in turn, he examines the array of possible outcomes compatible with that choice of strategy. There are $(n + 1)$ strategies available to the other $(m - 1)$ players, and "reality" has some enormous number, S, of possible social states available to it, so the array will consist of $S(n + 1)^{(m-1)}$ payoffs. But this array will *not* consist of a single state-of-nature value in all places but one. The actual distribution of values will be a bit more complicated. For each one of the S states of nature, there are $(n + 1)^{(m-1)}$ outcomes, corresponding to all of the ways in which the $m - 1$ other players can choose among the $n + 1$ strategies available to them. Some of these, n in number, will be coordinations on principles of justice, so for each possible state of nature there will be $[(n + 1)^{(m-1)} - n]$ identical outcomes, each with a value equal to the payoff *in that state of nature* to the worst-off individual, and n different outcomes, one for the value to the worst-off individual under each of the n principles as it is instantiated in that state of nature. Since there are S states of nature (a *very* large number!), there will be $S[(n + 1)^{(m-1)} - n] + Sn$ total outcomes, which, as it should, equals $S(n + 1)^{(m-1)}$; and there will be $S + Sn = S(n + 1)$ distinct outcomes in the entire array.

When a player runs his eye over the $S(n + 1)^{(m-1)}$ entries corresponding to a given strategy choice, he looks at all $S(n + 1)$ distinct entries and selects the absolutely smallest one. This, we may assume, will be the value to

158

the worst-off individual of the worst state of nature.[48] Since this value shows up in each of the $n + 1$ arrays corresponding to the player's strategy choices, it will be his maximum security level. As before, weak dominance will eliminate the state of nature option, and either cooperation or coordination holds out a reasonable hope of arriving at the difference principle as the unanimous strategy choice.

The purpose of this technical churning about has been to expose the assumptions underlying Rawls's informal and rather sketchy argument. A number of points are already clear. First, Rawls assumes that the players will, in the construction of the payoff matrix, be able to perform a number of exceedingly complex expected utility calculations; they may not know who they are or which society they are in, but that is just about *all* they don't know. Second, in the construction of the payoff matrix, the players are to adopt an *optimistic* attitude toward the bargaining process and are therefore to assign to each state of nature outcome the value of that state of nature to the worst-off person in it. Third, the players are to assume, without argument or serious consideration, that the official adoption of a principle guarantees its successful implementation. Alternatively, they are to assume, also without argument, that the difference principle is one of the principles that can in fact be successfully implemented in every possible state of nature. Fourth, once the payoff matrix is constructed according to Rawls's specifications, "maximin" seems to be irrelevant. Simple considerations of symmetry should suffice to lead

[48] It may be, but need not be, the state of nature operating at the lowest technological level to which the difference principle is intended to apply. In any case, we may be sure that it is pretty bad!

the players to coordination on, or cooperative agreement to, the difference principle.

Finally, and most important of all, the crucial step in Rawls's argument, the step in which he appeals to what he calls "maximin," the step that we have not yet subjected to critical scrutiny, is the *construction of the non-state-of-nature entries in the payoff matrix itself*. Although in his discussion of the subject, Rawls claims to be defending the maximin rule of choice under uncertainty in the special circumstances of the original position, he can in fact only be understood as defending a particularly pessimistic rule for deriving the payoff matrix from the outcome matrix. It is time, therefore, that we examine that defense, for on it depends whatever plausibility Rawls's entire theory may have.

The Construction of the Payoff Matrix

Although his treatment of the subject of "maximin" is lengthy and complex (see Sections 26–29 of *A Theory of Justice*), Rawls hedges and trims in a way that makes it extremely difficult to come to terms with his fundamental claims. In the opening pages of his discussion, for example, he says that "it is useful *as a heuristic device* to think of the two principles as the maximin solution to the problem of social justice. There is *an analogy* between the two principles and the maximin rule for choice under uncertainty" (p. 152, emphasis added). This might lead us to believe that Rawls does not really mean to invoke maximin in the strict game-theoretic sense; and yet his arguments and footnote references throughout the remainder of the three sections on the subject contain no such hesitations or qualifications.

Several pages later, in explaining his reasons for adopting maximin, Rawls denies that he is talking about *utility* in the sense that has become standard in game theory, welfare economics, and associated disciplines. "The essential point, though," he writes, "is that in justice as fairness the parties do not know their conception of the good and cannot estimate their utility in the ordinary sense. In any case, we want to go behind the de facto preferences generated by given conditions. Therefore expectations are based upon an index of primary goods and the parties make their choice accordingly" (p. 155). But this, as we shall see shortly, makes total hash out of two of his three reasons for adopting the maximin mode of reasoning.

At the risk of seeming to ignore the explicit disclaimers with which Rawls has filled his book, I propose to follow the same course here that I have followed elsewhere in this essay. I shall assume that Rawls *is* attempting to lay out and defend a formal argument, and I shall impute to him whatever formal machinery, utility functions and the rest, that his argument plainly presupposes.

Why adopt so pessimistic a rule in constructing the payoff matrix from the outcome matrix? In the very earliest form of the model, a player constructed his payoff matrix by means of complex expected utility calculations. Once the veil of ignorance is lowered, this course of action is no longer open to him. Since he does not know who he is or what his particular utility function is, he cannot estimate the likelihood of occupying this or that position in one or another social system governed by one of the available principles; nor can he determine how much the rewards of any such position would be worth to him. Thus far, the choice situation is simply indeterminate, and neither maximin nor any other rule of choice makes the slightest sense.

But Rawls provides the players with a knowledge of the basic facts of society, and that suffices to enable them

161

to construct the sort of $(m + 1)$-dimensional outcome matrix we have been discussing. Rawls also provides the players with a rough but serviceable utility function in the form of a theory of life-plans and primary goods. In a moment, we shall see that Rawls's argument implies a relatively "rectangular" exponential relationship between primary goods and utility, but, regardless of its precise shape, it should be clear that Rawls *is* committed to some conception of the players' utility function despite his disclaimers. He says that each player has a plan of life for which he requires quantities of primary goods, so we may assume that players are not indifferent to how much primary goods they get. Rawls implies that goods other than primary goods are of relatively little importance to a player (since otherwise it would be irrational for him to evaluate principles or outcomes purely in terms of primary goods payoffs), so we may conclude that each player's utility function, speaking roughly, is a function of the index of primary goods alone. We are told that primary goods are the sorts of things one wants more rather than less of, so we know that, for each player, utility is a monotonically increasing function of the index of primary goods. And, of course, since the theory of life-plans and primary goods is assumed to apply indifferently to every human being, and the players in the original position have no individuating information, all players have identically the same utility function. This last point suffices to make the payoff matrix symmetric, and so holds out hope of a solution.

But having said all that, why not permit the players to engage in expected utility calculations? To be sure, the calculations would all be identical, but the results would be quite different from the "worst off" calculations dictated by Rawls. Rawls offers three reasons for what we may call the rule of pessimism. As he says, acknowledg-

ing the controversiality of maximin, "there appear to be
three chief features of situations that give plausibility to
this unusual rule" (p. 154). These are:

> [T]he situation is one in which a knowledge of likelihoods
> is impossible, or at best extremely insecure. [p. 154]

> [T]he person choosing has a conception of the good such
> that he cares very little, if anything, for what he might
> gain above the minimum stipend that he can, in fact, be
> sure of by following the maximin rule. It is not worth-
> while for him to take a chance for the sake of a further
> advantage, especially when it may turn out that he loses
> much that is important to him. [p. 154]

> [T]he rejected alternatives have outcomes that one can
> hardly accept. The situation involves grave risks. [p. 154]

I am about to launch into an extended and, at times,
technical examination of these three reasons, but, before
we get mired in detail, it is worth recalling exactly what
is being debated. Despite Rawls's frequent remarks to
the contrary, the question before us is *not* what the morally admirable, or obligatory, or just, or fair choice of
principles would be for a player in the original position.
The question is what the rationally self-interested choice
would be. The conditions of the choice, including the
rules of the game and the combination of knowledge and
ignorance, are supposed to guarantee that a principle arrived at through cooperation or coordination by a group
of rationally self-interested players will *necessarily be*
morally admirable, obligatory, just, and fair. Rawls has a
tendency to blur this point, as we shall see in Section
XVI, but his entire theory rests on it, and so we must be
sure to hold him to it.

Consider first Rawls's claim that a knowledge of likelihoods is impossible, or at best extremely insecure. His
discussion seems to suggest that he has in mind the diffi-

culty of telling how a particular social reality would work itself out, as well as the impossibility of knowing which social reality the players are in and who each player is in that society. But Rawls's imputation to the players of a knowledge of the basic facts of society makes no sense at all unless they *are* able to make rough probability estimates of the workings of a given society. What else could it mean to say that they had knowledge? One might as well describe space travelers lost in space as knowing the "general facts of nature," and then say that they would have no idea whether it was going to be pleasant or painful to bump into a star!

Quite clearly, what Rawls thinks the players cannot estimate is what society they are in and who they are in it. Now, the first of these is no problem so far as the construction of the payoff matrix is concerned. As we have seen, the players are to compute a different value for each possible state of society. The possibility or impossibility of estimating which one they are in will indeed re-enter after the matrix is constructed, but we can put that problem off for a bit.

As for the impossibility of estimating who one is in a given society, Rawls here relies on the well-known objections to what is sometimes called "the principle of insufficient reason." The idea is this: if I want to determine the probability that a die will come up four, and if I have no idea at all what the die is likely to do, I might be tempted to suppose that since there are six possible outcomes (six faces of the die), and since I have insufficient reason to suppose any one of them more probable than any other, the correct probability assignment is 1/6. But I can equally well suppose that there are four possible outcomes, namely a 2, a 4, a 6, or an odd number; with insufficient reason to assign one of those outcomes a higher probability than any other, I conclude that the probability is 1/4. I can also view the situation as one in which a four either will or will not turn up, so the probability, following the same rule, must be 1/2. And so on. Thus, it appears that the law of insufficient reason, as a principle for assigning probabilities, leads to contradictions.

The usual reaction to examples of this sort is to state, "But look here! The *natural* way to divide things up is to say that there are six outcomes, corresponding to the six faces. Any other way is just gimmicky and irrelevant." But we want to say that only because we already think we know that each of the faces is equally likely to turn up! If we *really* are ignorant of the probabilities of various outcomes, then we have no way of knowing what the proper classification of outcomes is. Or, to put the same point differently, our classification is simply a summation of our beliefs about the situation, so we cannot divide the outcomes up and then blandly deny that we know which of them is more likely.

In the bargaining game, a player's first thought might be that it is equally probable that he will be any one of the people in any of the societies in which he might end up. Such reasoning will lead him to some sort of expected utility calculation. But Rawls rejects this move. There seem to be "no objective grounds in the initial situation for assuming that one has an equal chance of turning out to be anybody" (p. 168). So, he concludes a page later, "I shall assume that the parties discount likelihoods arrived at solely on the basis of this principle. This supposition is plausible in view of the fundamental importance of the original agreement and the desire to have one's decision appear responsible to one's descendants who will be affected by it" (p. 169). The reference to one's descendants, I think, is simply irrelevant, and the seriousness of the decision has already been taken fully into account in the construction of the universal utility function, as we shall see. So it comes down to the reasonableness of invoking the principle of insufficient reason.[49]

I should like to suggest that this is one case in which that principle is peculiarly appropriate. Consider the situation. A player knows that he is one of m players, but he does not know how large or small the number m is. (If he did, he would have a clue as to the character of the society from which he came.) He knows that these m players, including himself, are already organized into a society and that all and only the adult members of that society are players in the game. (It would be unfair to bar anyone from the game, or to permit visitors from another society to play the game for a lark.) He knows, too (and this is crucial), that the relevant division of the society

[49] John Harsanyi has pointed out that the extreme pessimism of the maximin rule is mathematically equivalent to one particular assignment of probabilities to the outcomes, namely that assignment in which the entire weight is placed upon the outcome with the lowest payoff. As utility theory is usually developed, a rational decision maker is assumed to exhibit behavior that obeys a set of powerful but plausible postulates. It is then shown that one can represent that behavior as equivalent to the maximizing of expected utility, the utility assignments to outcomes being invariant up to a linear transformation. As Harsanyi puts it, a decision maker whose behavior conforms to the postulates "*cannot help* acting *as if* he tried to maximize his expected utility, computed on the basis of some set of subjective probabilities" (Harsanyi, *APSR*, Vol. 69, No. 2 [June 1975], 599). If a player in Rawls's game adopts maximin, he can either be construed as assigning probability 1 to the worst outcome; or he can be construed as assigning the largest interval permitted by his utility scale to the gap between the worst alternative and the next to worst; but he *cannot* be construed both as assigning a probability measurably less than 1 to the worst alternative and also as assigning it a value commensurable with that of the other alternatives. In the axiomatic treatment of utility, to exhibit the choice behavior summarized as "the rule of maximin" just *is* to make probability or value assignments in that way.

under consideration is into individual persons. Rawls's moral framework guarantees that. So there are m players; each of them is one of the m persons in the society which they inhabit; the relevant question is how primary goods shall be distributed among those m persons; and for each of the S societies to which a player may actually belong, there is a rough class structure or distribution pattern *which he knows*. (He knows, for example, that in an advanced industrial capitalist society, the income structure is pyramidal, not inversely pyramidal—that is a basic fact of society if anything is!) What possible reason can a player have for *not* supposing that he has a $1/m$ chance of turning out to be each of the m persons in his society?

We come then to the second and third reasons for "pessimism." Taken together, they add up to the claim that the universal utility function in terms of which each player evaluates outcomes has a "rectangular" shape something like that of the curve in Figure 6.

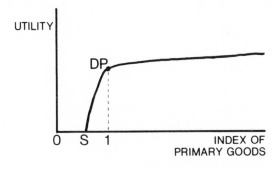

FIGURE 6

There is a natural zero-point on the utility axis, namely the point corresponding to a quantity of primary goods, S, not quite sufficient for survival. Since players, we may assume, are indifferent among the various ways

167

in which they fail to survive, that point is the absolute minimum of the curve. As the index of primary goods rises, the utility curve rises sharply; life gets markedly better. Finally, a point is reached beyond which (taking everything else into account, including the priority of liberty, etc.) a player "cares very little, if anything, for what he might gain." The curve therefore flattens out dramatically, albeit still rising, since players have positive marginal utility for primary goods. The point DP may be imagined as the point at which the slope of the curve is 1. We can arbitrarily set the quantity of primary goods corresponding to that point equal to one unit.

Now suppose that we were to offer a player a gamble: the certainty of one unit of primary goods, which will place him at point DP on his utility curve, or a 50-50 chance of either a gain of q units of primary goods or a loss of r units. (r will obviously have to be smaller than $1 - S$.) This is a situation carrying "grave risks," as Rawls puts it, for from the shape of the curve it is obvious that a rather small loss, r, of primary goods will cost the player more utility than even a very large gain, q.

But now take a look at Figure 7. If a player is at point

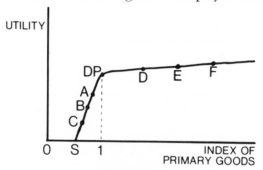

FIGURE 7

B on his utility curve, then he may very well be willing to enter into an attractive looking gamble between points *A* and *C* rather than settle for the certainty of *B*. The reason is that the slope of the curve makes the amounts of primary goods that he must gain to move up from *B* to *A* somewhere in the same order of magnitude as the amount he must lose to move down from *B* to *C*. The same is true for a gamble of *D* or *F* versus the certainty of *E*, save that in that case there is much less utility at stake. Only at point *DP* and points very near it on either side will it be true, as Rawls's argument requires, that the certainty of *DP* is preferable to any plausible, non-astronomical gamble between a gain, *q*, and a loss, *r*, of primary goods.

With a utility curve of this shape, a player now sets about constructing his payoff matrix from the outcome matrix. If this analysis is correct, then we may construe a Rawlsian player as reasoning in the following manner:

For each possible society, I must assign a value corresponding to the adoption in that society of each of the available principles. Let me start by considering society S_1. From my knowledge of the basic facts of society, I know that in a society of that sort, principle 1 will result in the formation of a certain system of social classes, divided into roughly the following proportions and receiving roughly the following index of primary goods. Since the principle of insufficient reason can be used here [This is me talking, not Rawls, of course], I can carry out an expected utility calculation and arrive at a value to be plugged into the payoff matrix. But wait a moment: some of the classes in this society will, under this principle, fall to the right of DP on the utility curve; others will fall to the left. Given the shape of that curve, a rather small change in my estimate of the relative sizes of those classes, or of their primary goods incomes, could result in a dramatic shift in the expected utility summation. I have

169

placed the middle class slightly to the right of DP. *But suppose I am a little wrong, and they are instead a bit to the left of* DP. *Considering the rough and ready nature of my calculations, even though I do know the basic facts of society, there is certainly a good chance that I may have erred in that way. There are clearly grave risks here, and this is not just an academic exercise in econometrics—this is my life! I had better play it safe, and choose as the value to be assigned to this outcome the utility expected by the worst off representative man.*

So long as the player computes the values of the outcomes in this manner, the difference principle must yield at least as good a string of numbers (for the various states of society) as any other principle. The result is a payoff matrix that, for the reasons of symmetry discussed above, will lead rational players to cooperate on or coordinate on the difference principle.

But now that we have spelled out the shape of the curve and the details of the reasoning, it should be obvious that a player will do as Rawls proposes only for a certain limited combination of possible societies and principles. So long as the payoffs for a particular society/ principle pair seem to group themselves around *DP*, so that slight errors in estimation will produce very great shifts in an expected utility calculation, extreme caution (or pessimism) may be justified. If the payoffs range themselves along only one side of *DP*, however, the reasoning underlying Rawls's "maximin" collapses. And if the payoff matrix is *not* constructed entirely along Rawls's pessimistic lines, then cooperation or coordination can *not* be expected to lead to the adoption of the difference principle. It will no longer necessarily be the case that, in each of the arrays associated with a social reality, the entry corresponding to the adoption of the difference principle is larger than any other.

As any reader of *A Theory of Justice* knows, there is not a word in the book to support the claim that any particular society, under the governance of some specific principle, will group its social classes around the point *DP*. But this much is clear: if the payoffs *are* so grouped for *some* society/principle combinations, then we may be sure that they will *not be* for many other society/principle combinations. It will therefore not be rationally prudent for a player to construct the payoff matrix in the manner assumed by Rawls; and there is therefore no reason whatsoever to suppose that the players in the bargaining game will coordinate or cooperate on the difference principle, or any other principle.

Technical Envoi

Just to nail the argument down tight, let us go back and consider the bargaining game after the payoff matrix has been constructed along the lines I have just suggested, rather than in Rawls's manner. If we accept the implications of symmetry without dispute, we can reduce the game to a simple game against nature played by a single player. (See pp. 139–40.) The payoff matrix is two-dimensional, showing all of the possible social states along one dimension and all of the available principles (including the state of nature option) along the other. Had we constructed the payoff matrix as Rawls directs, simple weak dominance would lead to the choice of the difference principle. But if we construct the matrix in the way I have outlined, using the rule of pessimism for society/principle combinations whose payoffs cluster around the point *DP* on the utility curve, and making expected utility estimates otherwise, then almost certainly no principle will weakly dominate any other. At this point, Rawls might be tempted to appeal to maximin in the true sense, locating the security level of each row and then choosing the strategy with the maximum security level. But this will yield the difference principle *only* if the technologically poorest society clusters its payoffs around *DP*. In that case, the rule of pessimism will dictate that the value for each principle be the utility of the worst-off individual; the difference principle will, under those circumstances, yield the highest value; and we may assume for simplicity that for any principle, the values of richer social states will be higher. As the reader may verify by drawing a sample payoff matrix along these lines, maximin does indeed then lead to the difference principle. BUT: if some of the social states cluster their payoffs all to the left of *DP* (a point, let us recall, that is objectively defined independently of social states), then very probably the security level of the difference principle will *not* be the maximum security level, and some other principle will be chosen by maximin. If he were to accept this analysis, Rawls could, I suppose, arbitrarily rule out social states whose payoffs fall to the left of *DP*, roughly in the way that Mill, in *On Liberty*, exempts the developing third world from the strictures of liberty and self-determination. But since questions of justice are particularly pressing left of *DP*, that would be an unfortunate move.

THE SHAPE OF THE UTILITY CURVE, AND OTHER MATTERS

Why should we suppose that a party in the original position has a conception of the good such that he cares very little, if anything, for what he can gain above some point *DP*? Is it plausible that the typical utility function will have the shape of the curves in Figures 6 and 7? I think not. The theory of life-plans and primary goods requires that the parties in the original position have secular, non-ascetic goals and tastes. Because they have rational plans of life, they do not live for the moment, sating themselves sensually with nary a thought for the morrow. Now, the fact of the matter is that, in a society like ours, the really expensive goods, the goods requiring a high index of primary goods, are for the most part the sorts of goods that would be desired by someone with a rational life plan rather than by an eat-drink-and-be-merry Cyrenaic. A full belly of beer and pizza requires very little money, but a cultivated, tasteful, elegant life-style, rationally managed in order to "schedule activities so that various desires can be fulfilled without interference," costs a bundle. If I knew that I had a life-plan of that sort, and if I knew the basic facts of society, then I would expect my utility curve to slope up rather markedly even after the flattening out had begun. Were I already assured of a payoff somewhere in the flattened range of the curve, I might reasonably take a few risks of falling below that point in order to improve my chances of moving to the right.

So far we have been concentrating solely on the portion of the curve to the right of the point DP. What of the portion to the left? Let us grant Rawls, for the sake of argument, that the curve slopes upward very steeply in that portion of it. Even so, its shape need not so terrify the players as to drive them into a Rawlsian pessimism. The reason, oddly enough, is suggested by Rawls himself in the midst of a discussion of possible objections to maximin. One familiar objection is the fact that the difference principle forces us to choose a course of action that guarantees a higher minimum payoff, no matter how slightly it exceeds the minima offered by alternative courses of action, and no matter how greatly the other possible payoffs of the alternatives exceed the other payoffs of the course of action chosen. Somewhat crudely, if action A guarantees $1, at worst, but offers only $1.01 at best, while action B guarantees $0.99 at worst and $1,000,000 at best, then maximin dictates that I choose action A.

To this, Rawls replies that the difference principle "is not intended to apply to such abstract possibilities." The entire passage is worth quoting:

> As I have said, the problem of social justice is not that of allocating *ad libitum* various amounts of something, whether it be money, or property, or whatever, among given individuals. Nor is there some substance of which expectations are made that can be shuffled from one representative man to another in all possible combinations. The possibilities which the objection envisages cannot arise in real cases; the feasible set is so restricted that they are excluded. The reason for this is that the two principles are tied together as one conception of justice which applies to the basic structure of society as a whole. The operation of the principles of equal liberty and open positions prevents these contingencies from occurring. For as we raise the expectations of the more advantaged the situation of the worst off is continuously improved. Each such increase is in the latter's interest, up to a certain point anyway. For the greater expectations of the more favored presumably cover the costs of training and encourage better performance thereby contributing to the general advantage. While nothing guarantees that inequalities will not be significant, there is a persistent tendency for them to be levelled down by the increasing availability of educated talent and ever widening opportunities. The conditions established by the other principles insure that the disparities likely to result will be much less than the differences that men have often tolerated in the past. [157–58]

The reader may be excused for feeling a slight vertigo

174

at Rawls's bland denial that any notion of shuffling money, or property, or whatever among representative men lies at the heart of his theory. All that talk about maximizing, all those quasi-economic graphs, with their implicit assumptions of continuity, divisibility, and the like, would certainly entice the unwary reader into such an interpretation. But for our purposes, the crux of this passage is the claim that the other two portions of the principles, the equal liberty and open positions clauses, have ruled out a number of imaginable patterns of distribution whose availability might cast doubt on the rationality of maximin.

The purpose of the passage is to show that the best-rewarded positions will not be fantastically better rewarded than the least. But the same sort of reasoning could as easily lead us to conclude that the least-well-rewarded positions will not be disastrously less-advantaged without maximin than with it. Equal liberty places significant constraints on how badly off the least well off member of a society may be permitted to be, as well as on how well off those at the top may be. The principle of "open positions," interpreted by Rawls to mean "fair equality of opportunity," also significantly ameliorates the condition of those on the low end of the social spectrum.

In light of these considerations, there is some reason to suppose that the operation of Principle I and Principle IIb will, by itself, rule out as unfeasible those ranges to the left of *DP*, fear of which might lead a player to adopt Rawls's pessimistic mode of evaluating outcomes. At the same time, the arguments in the passage quoted above, while certainly suggesting that jackpot payoffs attractive to natural gamblers would be excluded from the feasible set, in no way suffice to establish the much stronger claim that a party "has a conception of the good such that

175

he cares very little, if anything, for what he might gain above the minimum stipend that he can, in fact, be sure of by following the maximin rule" (154).

One final point concerning the appeal of maximin. Somewhat further on, in the section entitled "The Main Grounds for the Two Principles of Justice," Rawls appeals to the facts of moral psychology, and to the problem of stability in the society established on the principles chosen in the original position, to buttress his case for maximin. In the full elaboration of his theory, one of the constraints that Rawls places upon the choice of principles is that they not be principles that the parties would find it hard to stick to in the real world. More precisely, the laws of human psychology, available in the original position, must encourage the parties to believe that there will be no excessive "strains of commitment" on themselves once they re-emerge into the real world and find themselves living under the principles they have chosen. According to this line of argument, those at the bottom of the society will have a very hard time accepting inequalities that benefit the upper classes by *dis*advantaging them. If one finds oneself holding the short end of the stick, Rawls suggests, it will be of little comfort to reflect that one gambled and lost. Hence a strain will be placed on the lower classes' commitment to the principles of the society, a strain that will undermine social stability.[50] But surely the very same point can be made about those who emerge from the veil to find that they are among the ablest, most energetic, and most productive members of the society. Will they not regret

[50] Here, as elsewhere, Rawls's argument bears a striking resemblance to Plato's argument in the *Republic*. What Plato calls "temperance," the willing acceptance by each class of its appropriate role in the social division of labor, corresponds to Rawls's notion of stability and well-orderedness.

that they chose so cautious and conservative a principle of distribution? And will this not place strains on their commitment to that principle?[51]

THE BARGAINING GAME AND
PURE PROCEDURAL JUSTICE

When Rawls introduces the veil of ignorance, he asserts that "the idea of the original position is to set up a fair procedure so that any principles agreed to will be just" (136). He goes on to explain that "the aim is to use the notion of pure procedural justice as the basis of the theory" (136). The analysis of the distinctions among imperfect, perfect, and pure procedural justice is one of the many lovely bits of philosophical reasoning with which *A Theory of Justice* is filled. The point, familiar to any reader of Rawls, is that, in the case of perfect or imperfect procedural justice, we have a criterion for determining the right or just outcome of a procedure independently of the procedure. We can then judge whether the procedure always, usually, rarely, or never produces the objectively correct result. In the case of pure procedural justice, on the other hand, the justice of the outcome consists entirely in the fact that fair procedures have been employed. Many alternative outcomes—indeed, perhaps every possible outcome—can under the right circumstances be purely procedurally just, and under the wrong circumstances be purely procedurally unjust. Trial by combat, assuming the existence of an attentive God, is an example of perfect procedural justice; trial by jury, given the fallibility of the human spirit, is an example of imperfect procedural justice; a fair lottery is an example of pure procedural justice.

[51] For an elaborate and detailed discussion of the subject, including this point, see Nozick, *Anarchy, State, and Utopia*, pp. 189ff.

Now, the crucial fact about pure procedural justice is that the fairness is in the doing. As Rawls says, "A distinctive feature of pure procedural justice is that the procedure for determining the just result must actually be carried out" (86). If the fairness of the two principles of justice consists in the fact that they are the outcome of a purely procedurally just bargaining game, then that bargaining game must in fact be carried out in order for the principles to be just. (Or, perhaps one ought to say, in order for those principles to be the principles of justice. There is a rather significant difference, but Rawls appears to confuse the two.)

But now we encounter a curious paradox. The outcome of a game is certain, and can be known in advance, if and only if there is no need to play the game and the outcome cannot be described as an instance of pure procedural justice. If Rawls were proposing, for example, that the unequally rewarded positions in society be assigned by a lottery, then clearly in order to make the assignment *fair* it would be necessary actually to hold the lottery. We would not be impressed by a judge who handed out the favored positions to his friends and then justified his behavior by pointing out that such a distribution *could* have resulted from a fair spin of the wheel!

So Rawls must choose: either he can claim that the bargaining game is *not* an example of pure procedural justice, or fairness, in which case he is free to try to prove that one particular outcome—the choice of the difference principle—will occur; or he can claim that the bargaining game *is* an example of pure procedural justice, in which case he cannot in principle claim to know in advance how the game will turn out.

I think it is clear that there really is no genuine appeal to the notion of pure procedural justice in Rawls's full-scale version of his theory. This impression is powerfully

178

strengthened by the Kantian interpretation of the original position, which we examined in Part Three. The kingdom of ends, as described in the *Groundwork of the Metaphysic of Morals*, is an aggregation of rational agents who do not in any essential way communicate with one another. Each agent rationally and autonomously wills the same fundamental principle of morality, and there is therefore no element of pure procedural justice in the legislation of the Categorical Imperative. Rawls has, by the transformations of his theory, undermined the logic of its justification and deprived it of one of its more attractive features.

I return, by way of the extended reasoning of this section, to the claim I made in the opening sections. The heart of Rawls's philosophy is the idea of the bargaining game, by means of which the sterility of Kant's formal reasoning was to be overcome, and a principle was to be established that would combine the strengths and avoid the weaknesses of utilitarianism and intuitionism. The idea is original, powerful, and elegant, but it simply does not stand up. The original sketch of the bargaining game was comprehensible, but it was open to crushing objections. The device of the veil of ignorance enables Rawls at least initially to avoid the pitfalls of the first model while seeming to link his philosophy to that of Kant. But the move is ultimately fatal, for in striving for absolute universality, for a contemplation of the foundations of social philosophy *sub specie aeternitatis*, Rawls abstracts from all that is characteristically human and social. The result is a model of a choice problem that is not sufficiently determined to admit of solution, and neither historical nor human enough to bear a useful relationship to the real issues of social theory. In Part Five, I shall try to say what other avenues I think it might be more fruitful for social theory to explore.

179

XVI

The Logical Status of Rawls's Argument

THE story is told of the great medievalist Harry
Austryn Wolfson that, when it came time for him
to retire after nearly half a century of teaching at Harvard, President Nathan Pusey asked him whom Harvard
could find to replace him. "Well," Wolfson is reputed to
have said, "in the first place, you will need three
people." When one confronts the question, "What is the
logical status of Rawls's argument?" the thought that
comes to mind is, "Well, first of all, you will need three
answers." Rawls attempts to unite them in his doctrine
of reflective equilibrium, but the truth is, I think, that
he really has three answers, and they do not entirely fit
together.

The first answer is the liveliest, the most original, the
boldest, and the most open to criticism.[52] It is that the
two principles of justice are the solution, in the strict
sense, of a bargaining game, the terms of which embody
a minimal notion of practical reason together with the
so-called conditions of justice, plus the single additional
premise that the players are prepared to make a once-
for-all commitment to a set of principles for the evaluation of practices, the principles to be chosen unanimously on the basis of rational self-interest. In the proof
of this proposition, "we should strive for a kind of moral
geometry with all the rigor which this name connotes"

[52] In view of the line Rawls takes in his very early paper, "An Out-
line of a Decision Procedure in Ethics," which appeared in *Philosophical Review* in 1951, we cannot also say that it was the first answer to occur to him.

(121). By virtue of the characteristics of the bargaining game, the solution is guaranteed to be just, so that the actual play of the game is an instance of pure procedural justice. To the question, Why ought we to govern our affairs in the manner specified by the principles of justice?, we can then answer either, Because those were the principles chosen in a fair bargaining game by persons (including yourself) suitably situated, or Because those are the principles that would be chosen in any fair bargaining game by persons like yourself suitably situated. The power of such a theorem would lie in the paucity of its premises. Specifically, the only premise to which a rational egoist (or a devotee of a competing morality) might object is the agreement to make a binding commitment to a set of principles. If the theorem could be proved, Rawls would then be in a position to say to a critic, "Either acknowledge that you are utterly unprincipled, and that by your refusal to acknowledge any principles you forfeit the respect owed to a moral being; or else grant that my two principles of justice are the principles to which you, as a rational agent, must be prepared to commit yourself."

That's not a bad challenge to fling in the face of one's adversaries. But alas, the theorem cannot be proved, not even with the countless adjustments, emendations, revisions, and bolsterings that we have chronicled throughout this essay. So Rawls must move instead to his second answer, which is a rather complex version of what might be called the "rational reconstruction" of ordinary moral consciousness.

A rational reconstruction is a systematization and analysis of a body of firmly held convictions that reveals the logical interconnections among them, and exhibits them as inferences from, or applications of, or in some sense derivatives from some small set of general principles. For example, utilitarianism can be construed as a rational reconstruction of a body of moral convictions designed to show that they are all injunctions to choose the act that promises to produce the greatest happiness for the greatest number. So too, the doctrine of the mean can be understood as a reconstruction of a number of settled evaluations of persons and character traits, revealing them all to have the form of a praise of the mean and a condemnation of the extremes in some species or other of human action.

A rational reconstruction is by no means a simple procedure, nor is it slavishly subservient to every detail of the moral convictions that are its starting point. In the course of systematizing my convictions, I might discover unsuspected inconsistencies or incoherences, and I might thereby be led materially to alter my beliefs. It is roughly such a process that leads reasonable people to give up unexamined prejudices.

One familiar example of the several-staged rational reconstruction is the progression from simple utilitarianism, through average utilitarianism, to rule-utilitarianism. In each case, the unacceptable moral implications of the general principles formulated at the previous stage force a revision that leads to a new reconstruction, whose principles achieve a better fit with the convictions of those carrying out the reconstruction.

So long as we remain in the realm of rational reconstruction, the logical status of the project is clear, and not terribly satisfactory. The ground for asserting the principles arrived at by the analysis is merely the general agreement of the audience with the original moral convictions of the author. In short, the entire procedure can do no more than aim for a sophisticated rendering of the *consensus gentium*. Needless to say, a moral theory of this sort has no defense against the moral skeptic, and it does not even have an argument to persuade those who sincerely and thoughtfully reject some of the key convictions on which the reconstruction rests.

The natural tendency, therefore, is to seek some independent proof of the first principles, once they have been identified and formulated by means of the reconstruction. Probably the best example of this move from reconstruction to proof is to be found in Kant's *Groundwork of the Metaphysic of Morals*. In Chapter One, Kant explicitly tells us that his intention is to reveal the presence of the categorical imperative in the ordinary moral judgments that he could expect his audience to share with him. In Chapter Two, he begins again with an analysis of willing and practical reason, and seeks to derive from that analysis the same principle that he has already extracted from moral assumptions in the first chapter. Kant is perfectly clear that his enterprise is valueless unless he can provide that derivation.

From the very start, Rawls has been torn between a desire to deduce the principles of justice as the solution to his bargaining game—and thereby to establish that they are, in a very strong sense, a priori principles of practical reason—and a belief that the most he can hope to accomplish is a far-reaching analysis of his settled social and moral convictions that will exhibit his two principles as a successful rational reconstruction of them.

There are three major difficulties with the strong a priori argument embodied in the bargaining-game version of Rawls's theory. First of all, as we have seen, Rawls cannot prove the theorem on which the argument rests, and as he himself frequently acknowledges, the obstacles in the way of proving such a theorem appear formidable. But second, there is considerable philosophical dispute over just what are the marks of "practical rationality." Is maximization of expected utility a noncontroversial principle of rational choice under risk? Hardly, when one considers the literature on the reasonableness of aversion to risk. Ought a rational agent to choose maximin, or some form of the principle of insufficient reason, or what Leonard Savage calls the principle of "minimax regret," or one of the many other principles that have been proposed as rules for choice under uncertainty?[53] Is the demand for complete orderings of available alternatives the weakest imaginable criterion of instrumental rationality, as most literature on rational choice assumes, or is A. K. Sen right in suggesting that various partial orderings and quasi-orderings more accurately reflect our moral intuitions?[54] Rawls's awareness of these disputes weakens his confidence in the self-evident acceptability of any particular formalization of the principles of formal rationality. Hence he is considerably less secure that his theorem, could it be proved, would settle the issue of social justice.

And finally, there remains the residual question, so what? Even if a satisfactory characterization of formal rationality can be fielded, and the two principles can be established as the solution, in a suitably strong sense, of a problem in collective choice, why should that fact persuade us to adopt the two principles as the fundamental criteria for the evaluation or correction of our social institutions?

As we have seen, Rawls substantially revises his model of the bargaining game in response to the first two of these sorts of criticisms. By the time the veil of ignorance has been imposed, together with the knowledge assumptions, the thin theory of the good, and the notion of plans of life; by the time the two principles have been

[53] Cf. Luce and Raiffa, *Games and Decisions*, Chapter 13.

[54] See Amartya K. Sen, *On Economic Inequality* (Oxford at Clarendon Press, 1973).

suitably altered, both by the imposition of priority rules and by the revision of the difference principle, and the extremely conservative rule of pessimism has been stipulated as the appropriate principle for constructing the payoff matrix; by that time, much of the initial dramatic plausibility of Rawls's key idea has been drained away. As for the third objection, its real force derives from the fact that Rawls's model, even in its purest form, is still a model of generalized heteronomy rather than autonomy. Hence for at least some significant moral philosophers it would fail entirely to capture the essence of the distinctively moral.

But despite these serious weaknesses of the bargaining-game version of the theory, Rawls persists in believing (rightly, I think) that a successful carrying through of such a project would be a genuinely powerful contribution to moral and social philosophy. So he is clearly unwilling simply to give up the effort and shift instead to rational reconstruction. The result of this ambivalence is the distinctive notion of "reflective equilibrium."

Rawls's account of reflective equilibrium (Section 4, "The Original Position and Justification") is elaborate and detailed, and nothing would be gained by summarizing his remarks here. The notion has been subjected to searching analysis by a number of authors.[55] The central idea, so far as I can understand it, is to carry out a rational reconstruction leading not only to a set of principles (in this case, the two principles of justice) but also to a model of rational choice. The model is then to be adjusted to the reconstruction in order that it can plausibly be construed as yielding the principles as the solution to

[55] See especially, Ronald Dworkin, "The Original Position," reprinted from the *Chicago Law Review*, in *Reading Rawls*, edited by N. Daniels.

a choice problem posed in terms of its formal structure. The model itself is to be argued for as having some independent merit as an account of the presuppositions of rational choice. This merit in turn lends some sort of support to the product of the reconstruction, over and above whatever support it derives from the truth of the settled convictions that were the starting point of the entire process of reconstruction. The result is not so much a proof as an anatomical dissection of the body of "our" moral opinions. The fact that the two principles would be chosen by parties in the original position strengthens our confidence in and deepens our understanding of those principles; the fact that those principles would be chosen in the sort of original position eventually sketched out by the theory in its full development strengthens in turn our belief that we have formulated the conditions of the original position correctly. Merely to reconstruct our convictions in the form of two principles for which we could find no independent support whatsoever would leave us uncertain whether we had articulated our morals or our prejudices. But to hunt for an a priori proof of those principles, by means of a purely analytic, noncontroversial explication of the bare form of practical reason, would be to follow Kant on a hopeless quest. So reflective equilibrium must suffice. And, Rawls clearly thinks, it does suffice, because nothing more could rationally be demanded of a moral philosopher or a reasonable citizen. Or so Rawls says. I persist in believing that, deep in his heart, he longs for the theorem, the proof from undoctored premises to undeniable conclusions.

But reflective equilibrium is only the second answer to our original question, What is the logical status of Rawls's argument? The third answer is more complex yet, involving as it does an extended series of speculations about the political institutions, child-rearing practices, and social arrangements that tends to support the parties in their real-world commitment to the principles that they are imagined to have chosen in the original position. Having adjusted the original position to fit the principles arrived at by the rational reconstruction, and having adjusted the principles in turn to make them the sorts of principles that parties in the original position would choose, Rawls now adjusts both the principles and the original position in order to yield results that would, if put into effect in the real world, encourage people to be the sorts of citizens who would naturally and willingly cooperate in and support the institutions dictated by the suitably tailored choice problem. The result of this final complication is to make the status of Rawls's claims so complex that I am utterly uncertain what is premise and what conclusion, what is argued for and what is being argued from.

One example illustrates the difficulty. It will be recalled that, from the very beginning, the players, or parties, in the original position are presumed not to be envious. As I have pointed out, the original purpose of the non-envy assumption is to make the appeal to an inequality surplus feasible. This is a significant restriction on the utility functions of the players, not called for by the bare formal requirements of practical reason. There is in general nothing irrational in caring about how others are getting along, and though it may be reprehensible to wish others ill rather than well, it does not seem to violate the canons of practical reason. So here we have an example of an adjustment of the model to make it yield the desired principles. Assuming that the two principles accord with our intuitions about just inequalities of distribution, we may also view this as an example of the suitability of the principles conferring merit on a detail of the model.

In the late Section 80, "The Problem of Envy," however, Rawls presents a very different line of argument. "The reason why envy poses a problem," Rawls says, is "the fact that the inequalities sanctioned by the difference principle may be so great as to arouse envy to a socially dangerous extent" (531). We must determine, he continues, "whether the principles of justice, and especially the difference principle with fair equality of opportunity, is likely to engender too much destructive general envy" (531–32). Originally, the question of envy arose in connection with the motivation postulated for the parties in the original position; now it reappears in connection with the quite different question of the harmony and stability of a society organized along supposedly just lines. Rawls's rationale for this procedure is worth looking at in detail:

> I have split the argument for the principles of justice into two parts: the first part proceeds on the presumptions just mentioned [that the parties in the original position are not envious, have no special attitudes toward risk, etc.], and is illustrated by most of the argument so far; the second part asks whether the well-ordered society corresponding to the conception adopted will actually generate feelings of envy and patterns of psychological attitudes that will undermine the arrangements it counts to be just. At first we reason as if there is no problem of envy and the special psychologies; and then having ascertained which principles would be settled upon, we check to see whether just institutions so defined are likely to arouse and encourage these propensities to such an extent that the social system becomes unworkable and incompatible with human good. *If so, the adoption of the conception of justice must be reconsidered.* [530–31, emphasis added.]

So it appears that, in addition to bringing the definition of the original position into accord with the princi-

188

ples arrived at by a rational reconstruction of our moral opinions, through a process of reflective equilibrium, we must also adjust both to our empirical estimates of the stability and harmony of a society governed by such principles.

The logic of the situation is now extremely obscure. Consider the possibilities. Suppose we adopt the strong line implicit in the original conception of the model and assert that whatever principles emerge from the bargaining game will, on the grounds of pure procedural fairness, be *just*. Then we can reasonably argue that the set of admissible solution points in the bargaining space is constrained by considerations of feasibility. Any point (i.e., any set of principles) that cannot in fact be implemented will be eliminated from the bargaining game on the grounds that its adoption would amount in practice to a failure to agree to a solution at all.

If, however, we adopt the rational reconstructionist position that the principles of justice are the implicit skeletal structure of our ordinary reasoning about matters of social morality, then the fact that a society governed by such principles may be inherently unstable will be a cause for existential despair or stoic resignation, perhaps, but hardly a reason for altering our principles. After all, as the Grand Inquisitor reminds us, the truth is hard for men to bear, and a well-ordered society—a society governed by a publicly acknowledged conception of justice—might not be a stable or orderly place to live! There might be perpetual temptations to forsake the truth for false prophecies and comforting pseudo-religious panaceas.

But, finally, if we demand stability as one of the conditions of the just society, then and only then will we be justified in reasoning backward to principles whose implementation promises stability, and beyond that to a model of rational choice that builds into it psychological assumptions that, when carried through, lead to a stable society.

In a sense, Rawls has his argument reversed. *If* it is rational not to be envious, and to select the difference principle in the original position by means of rationally self-interested choice, then we will want a social system that cuts down on envy because we will recognize envy as irrational. We will judge it so because it is mutually harmful, consigning us to a condition that is Pareto-inferior to some other just and available state. But if it is not irrational to be envious, then we will not necessarily reject an otherwise mutually advantageous social system that engenders painful envy. We may view envy as a legitimate emotion, one which we wish to countenance, or even which we wish to stimulate in others.

The logical status of Rawls's theory is unclear, I suggest, because, in addition to his conception of rational choice and his settled moral convictions about particular matters of social justice, Rawls also has an extremely powerful commitment to an Idealist conception of the harmonious and organic society. Particularly in the latter portions of *A Theory of Justice*, this conception is brought heavily into play and assumes more and more of the weight of the argument. So, as I have observed, there are really three answers to the question, What is the logical status of Rawls's argument? The first answer is, It is a sketch of a proof of a theorem in the theory of collective rational choice. The second answer is, It is a complicated sort of rational reconstruction of the social and moral convictions of himself and (he hopes) his audience, in which some adjustment of the outcome of the reconstruction is made to fit it to the model of rational choice and to fit the model of rational choice to it. The third answer is, It is a vision of a harmoniously integrated, stable social and political order whose structure is articulated by the two principles of justice, which in turn are altered and adjusted in order to strengthen the hope that a society lived under their direction will in fact maintain its harmony and stability.

These three answers do not, in my judgment, cohere. The demands of each undermine the requirements of the other two. If the argument is to be the proof of a theorem, then the premises cannot endlessly be adjusted in the most ad hoc way to yield the intended consequences. If the argument is a rational reconstruction of our moral convictions, then no weight is lent to the resultant principles by a gerrymandered bargaining game, and considerations of stability and harmony will be irrelevant to the correctness of the reconstruction. Finally, if the argument is in truth an extended exposition of a social vision, as the concluding words of Rawls's book very strongly suggest, then the device of the bargaining game seems otiose, and the elaborate construction of the original position a mere holdover from an earlier stage of development.

XVII

The Abstractness of Rawls's Theory

IS Rawls right? Are *his* two principles really *the* principles of justice? Are they the principles in accordance
with which any society exhibiting the "conditions of justice" *ought* to arrange its practices and distribute the
rights and liberties, goods and services which its collective practices make possible or produce?

I find it extraordinarily difficult to get a grip on this
question, despite the care with which Rawls develops
subsidiary themes in his theory. The problem, in part,
stems from the fact that Rawls says little or nothing about
the concrete facts of social, economic, and political reality. For all the reasons I have chronicled throughout this
essay, (A *Theory of Justice* can be placed historically in
the tradition of utopian liberal political economy of the
late nineteenth and early twentieth centuries) One could
characterize it briefly, even brusquely, as a philosophical
apologia for an egalitarian brand of liberal welfare-state
capitalism. And yet the device of the bargaining game
and the veil of ignorance, while preserving the political,
psychological, and moral presuppositions of such a doctrine, raise the discussion to so high a level of abstraction
that the empirical specificity needed to lend any plausibility to it are drained away. What remains, it seems to
me, is ideology, which is to say prescription masquerad-
ing as value-neutral analysis.)

Many readers of *A Theory of Justice*, in an effort to
test its theses against their own moral or political intuitions, have thought up test cases in which the application
of the principles might have significant implications (it is

the difference principle—Principle IIa—that attracts most of the attention). Inevitably, these test cases are rather small-scale, for it would take the talents of a Dickens or a Tolstoy to conjure an entire society as an example, and the learning of a Weber to judge how such a society would work itself out.

As I have tried to show, the original formulation of the bargaining problem encourages small-scale, or micro-test cases; but in his book, (Rawls sets aside such thought-experiments, stipulating that his principles are to be applied only to the basic structure of a society as a whole) So, for example, we are simply to ignore as irrelevant the sorts of hypothetical choice-examples, easily representable by a two-by-two or three-by-two payoff matrix, in terms of which we can test our intuitions concerning the maximin rule for choice under uncertainty.[56] Some critics have complained—I think with justification—that by ruling out micro-tests in which our intuitions are strong and the multiplicity of factors conceptually manageable, Rawls has overprotected his theory to the point of vacuity.[57] Nevertheless, I agree with Rawls that the principles of social justice must be conceived, in the first instance, as applying to society as a whole rather than to small-scale practices from which a society can be aggregated. I am willing, therefore, to follow his lead, and to think about the two principles in their society-wide application.

Consider contemporary American society. The basic facts of income and wealth distribution are well-known and have been widely discussed in recent years. Putting it very roughly (since, for our purposes, nothing is to be

[56] See, for example, Harsanyi, *APSR*, Vol. 69, No. 2 (June 1975), p. 594. Also, p. 597.

[57] On this point, see Robert Nozick, *Anarchy, State, and Utopia*, pp. 204ff.

gained by a straining after precision), the lowest fifth of households, in terms of income, receives about 5 percent of the income distributed in a year, while the highest fifth receives about 40 percent—an eightfold spread. Even taking into account such mitigating facts as the larger number of single-person "households" in the lower fifths, it remains true that income is very unevenly distributed. Wealth, of course, is much more unevenly distributed than income. (The wealthiest one-half of 1 percent of all families own perhaps one-quarter of all the wealth, while the holdings of the lower 50 percent are negligible.) The data on income and wealth taken together, incidentally, dramatically show that it is income inequality rather than wealth inequality that accounts for the basic pattern of distribution in America. Save for the special case of large accumulations of capital, whose primary significance is as sources of economic power rather than as sources of private satisfaction, what matters most in America is how much your job pays, not how big your portfolio is or how much land you have inherited.[58]

I believe that the pattern of distribution of income and wealth in America is unjust (although I and my family are

[58] Since one often hears of sheltered millions on which little tax is paid, and proposals for income redistribution manage always to make it sound as though a few rich families are all that keep the other two hundred million of us down, it might be worth noting some of the actual dollar figures at which different fractions of the population divide from one another. In 1974, for example, a young husband and wife, each with a new Ph.D. and a job as an assistant professor at $14,500, could by teaching summer school just scrape into the top *five* percent of all American families (cutoff point: $31,948). If a union carpenter earning $7 an hour and his waitress wife pulling in $2.50 an hour in wages and tips could persuade their teenage son to mow lawns and bag groceries, and if their thirteen year old daughter did some regular babysitting one evening a week, the four of them would find themselves in the top fifth of American families (cutoff point $20,445). When we speak of soaking the rich, neither of these

clearly winners in it, not losers); and the tenor of Rawls's occasional remarks suggests that he agrees. How would he have us think about that injustice? How would he have us compare the present set of economic arrangements to other possible arrangements?

Presumably, we are to look at the reasonable expectations of the least advantaged representative household in our society and ask whether there is some other set of arrangements that would increase those expectations. Now, I have made much of Rawls's unclarity with regard to the indexing of primary goods, the defining of "least advantaged representative man," the lexical priority of political "goods," and so forth. But I propose to ignore any rhetorical advantage that might be gained by reactivating those criticisms here, because I believe that the problems in Rawls's social philosophy go a good deal deeper.

The first question to ask is whether there is an undistributed inequality surplus being generated in our economy by the existing set of economic arrangements.[59] If we assume that plumbers must be paid more than department store clerks in order to encourage young men

---

families comes readily to mind. In light of the actual figures (which may be found, for example, in the *Statistical Abstract of the United States*), it is difficult to see why Rawls imputes life-plans to parties in the original position that are of such a nature that they care little for what they may obtain, in the way of primary goods, above what they can secure through the difference principle. Anyone living in the United States today should have a keen sense of the difference in quality of life purchasable with, say $20,445 per family as against $14,916 (the top, or cutoff point, of the third fifth).

[59] In order to avoid begging any methodological or theoretical questions, I am using this neutral, and rather vague, locution, "set of economic arrangements," instead of such loaded phrases as "social relationships of production." Eventually, I shall want to argue that Rawls's way of talking abstracts from most of what is causally significant in the economic and political life of a society.

(and women, if Principle IIb is enforced) to train as plumbers, and in order to draw into plumbing those with a hydraulic turn of mind, must they be paid *as much more* than clerks as they now are? Speaking generally, could our present division of labor and pattern of wages be altered in the direction of equalizing rewards without making it unmanageable? Are there significant categories of higher paid workers whose income is greater than would be required to attract them to, sort them into, and hold them in, those better rewarded occupations?

Let us suppose that the answer to these questions is, and is known by us to be, yes. I believe it is, I think Rawls believes so too; and since my quarrel with him turns on other questions, I propose to avoid the treacherous quicksand of econometric estimations.

The second question we must ask, following the guidance of Rawls's principles, is whether there are other, entirely different sets of economic arrangements that, while serving the fundamental purposes of production and reproduction of goods and services, will generate inequality surpluses, the feasible distribution of which would raise the expectations of the least advantaged representative man above the level that can be achieved under our present arrangements by redistributing the existing inequality surplus. I apologize to the reader for the complexity of that sentence, but the question Rawls's theory requires us to ask is very complicatedly hypothetical. I can think of a number of different ways to organize the growing of wheat or the assembling of automobiles—both of which, however, are merely small-scale or micro-examples from Rawls's point of view. But when I try to form a usable notion of alternatives to our present total set of economic arrangements, my mind can do no better than to rehearse the arrangements that have actually existed in some society or other—feudalism, slave-labor farming, hunting and gathering, state capitalism, collectivist socialism, and so forth. After eliminating those arrangements (slavery, for example) that violate portions of Rawls's principles other than the difference principle, I am to imagine how each of the remaining candidates would work out under the conditions of technology, resource availability, and actual or potential labor skill level obtaining in America today. Then I must gauge the size (if any) of the inequality surplus thus generated, and estimate the effect of the most favorable feasible redistribution on the reasonable expectations of the least advantaged representative man. Finally, Rawls tells me to order all of the alternative sets of arrangements under consideration according to the magnitude of the expectations of the least advantaged. I now presumably know which alternatives are more just, and which less just, than present-day America, and the last step is simply to shift to the number-one candidate on the list.

The manifest vagueness of these calculations and estimations has a very important consequence for Rawls's theory. Inevitably, one finds oneself construing the difference principle as a pure distribution principle. One simply stops asking *how* the goods to be distributed actually come into existence. Robert Nozick puts the point very nicely when arguing for his own conception of the principles of justice against Rawls's approach:

> If things fell from heaven like manna, and no one had any special entitlement to any portion of it ["entitlement" is given a special meaning in Nozick's theory], and no manna would fall unless all agreed to a particular distribution, and somehow the quantity varied depending on the distribution, then it is plausible to claim that persons placed so that they couldn't make threats, or hold out for specially large shares, would agree to the difference principle of distribution. But is *this* the appropriate model for

thinking about how the things people produce are to be distributed?[60]

Rawls has replies to this sort of criticism. After all, he might point out, the difference principle does not posit a given, once-for-all bundle of goods and services that must be distributed. It applies to on-going practices in which unequal effort, talent, or what-have-you are already and legitimately rewarded unequally. The difference principle only requires that any *inequality surplus* be redistributed so as to maximize the expectations of the least advantaged. The theory takes fully into account—indeed, it must take into account—how goods and services are produced, and how the people who produce them would respond to changes in their rewards for that production.

But though Rawls might respond in that way, Nozick's criticism is well taken. The veil of ignorance has the effect of making all considerations on the production side so thoroughly hypothetical, so *abstract* in the bad sense, that inevitably the difference principle comes to be construed as a pure distribution principle, with the distributable goods and services exogenously given. It is hardly surprising that when other philosophers try to formalize the difference principle so that it can be given some sort of proof, they tend to treat it in that manner.[61]

[60] Nozick, *Anarchy, State, and Utopia*, p. 198.

[61] See, for example, the treatment by Amartya K. Sen, *Collective Choice and Social Welfare* (Holden-Day, 1970), Chapters 9 and 9*. See also Steven Strasnick, "Social Choice and the Derivation of Rawls' Difference Principle," *J. Phil.*, 73 (Feb. 26, 1976), pp. 85–99. Strasnick tries to transform the bargaining game into a collective choice problem à la Arrow, as in a sense does Sen. Strasnick gets his definitions confused, so that in fact his proof of his theorem is invalid, but even if he were to sort things out, it would remain the case that his treatment transforms the problem into a pure distribution problem. See my discussion, "Some Remarks Concerning Strasnick's 'Derivation' of Rawls' 'Difference Principle,' " scheduled to appear in the *Journal of Philosophy* in December 1976.

Even if we were able to carry out the calculations required by the two principles, it is not clear what significance we could attach to the results, because the principles bear no relationship at all to any coherent notion of socio-economic causation. Rawls seems to have no conception of the generation, deployment, limitations, or problems of political power. In a word, he has no theory of the *state.*

When one reflects that *A Theory of Justice* is, before all else, an argument for substantial redistributions of income and wealth, it is astonishing that Rawls pays so little attention to the institutional arrangements by means of which the redistribution is to be carried out. One need not know many of the basic facts of society to recognize that it would require very considerable political power to enforce the sorts of wage rates, tax policies, transfer payments, and job regulation called for by the difference principle. The men and women who apply the principle, make the calculations, and issue the redistribution orders will be the most powerful persons in the society, be they econometricians, elected representatives, or philosopher-kings. How are they to acquire this power? How will they protect it and enlarge it once they have it? Whose interests will they serve, and in what way will the serving of those interests consolidate them and strengthen them vis-à-vis other interests? Will the organization of political power differ according to whether the principal accumulations of productive resources are privately owned rather than collectively owned?

Questions of this sort have been the stock in trade of the political economist, political sociologist, and political philosopher for at least the two centuries since the publication of *The Wealth of Nations*, and, in a slightly different form, they constitute the conceptual skeleton for such classic works as Plato's *Republic*. Laissez-faire liberals, welfare-state neo-classicals, and democratic socialists will dispute about the answers, but all would agree that any theory of social justice must include some coherent account of the sources, organization, distribution, and workings of political power. Rawls, so far as I can see, has no such account.

Two answers to this charge come readily from the pages of *A Theory of Justice*. The lengthy discussions of stability and congruence and the excursions into moral psychology address precisely the issue of the individual's motivation to cooperate in the system of practices that has been established under the guidance of the two principles. And the explicit announcement, in the opening pages, that the theory is to apply to "well-ordered societies," finesses all of the objections my remarks are designed to raise. Well-ordering, Rawls might say, is akin to what Plato called the social virtue of "temperance" in the just society: it is the willing acceptance, by the citizens of the Republic, of the functionally differentiated roles the rational principle of justice has assigned to them in the good society. Rawls may have neglected to conjure for us, as Plato did, the ways in which, and by which, the good society can degenerate; but the Platonic theory of justice does not rest either evidentially or logically on that brilliant account of the decline of the ideal state, and Rawls's theory does not require any such addendum either.

To put the same point somewhat differently, Rawls might argue that we must first arrive at a satisfactory conception of how a society *ought* to arrange its practices and the associated distributions of primary goods, before we can determine how far our own society falls short of that ideal and what steps we ought to take to rectify our shortcomings. Without such a conception, we shall

forever be confusing disputes over principle with disagreements about details of institutional reorganization.

But replies of this sort would miss the deeper point at
issue. Rawls's theory of social justice is utopian in the
sense that the theories of the early French socialists
were utopian. His theory is, as I have already said,
"abstract," by which I mean that it abstracts from the
significant factors determining the nature and development of social reality. This abstractness is reflected in the models of analysis Rawls employs. The
problem is not that the models are "formal" or that they
are capable of being represented symbolically. Quite to
the contrary; any attempt to think about social reality
that eschewed such models would remain at the level of
anecdote. But there are good models and bad models, so
to speak, and the models of game theory, bargaining
theory, and welfare economics, on which Rawls relies,
are bad models for the analysis of social and economic
life.

A model is like a map (or, one might say, a map is a
particular sort of model with which we are all familiar). It
abstracts from most of the complex particularity of a state
of affairs or system of objects and events, simplifies and
thereby sharpens certain relationships, and presents
what remains in a manner that is easily grasped. The
value of a map is relative to the purposes for which it is
needed, and the same can be said for any model.

Suppose that I am in a forest (a state of nature, as it
were), and I want to go to one or another of several cities
that lie somewhere roundabout. I shall, of course, need
to know what those cities are like, so that I can judge
which of them I would prefer to make my way to. But I
shall also need a map showing me where those cities are
in relationship to my point in the forest. Now, a map
showing nothing more than directions and distances will

be very little help at all, for it will not tell me where the mountain ranges are, or where I can find manageable passes through them. It will fail to alert me to rivers, deserts, and tricky swamps. With such a map, I might mistakenly suppose that two cities were equally easy to reach, merely because they lay at equal distances from my starting point. Cities close together on the map might have no direct route from one to another, even though each could be got to from where I was.

Rawls's difference principle, I suggest, is a rule for constructing a "map" that has all the faults I have just described. It is a rule for constructing a social indifference map from which all significant historical, political, and social features have been removed. As a result, it represents points as being close to one another that might be all but unreachable one from the other, and separates points that might, in economic and political reality, lie virtually adjacent.[62]

Consider the following three possible sets of social arrangements and the way in which they might be ordered by the difference principle.

The first is a capitalist economy with a powerful state, a large public sector, very wide divergences of income, and well-established institutions of formal democracy but considerable inequality in the distribution of actual political power among the major economic groups (in short, the United States today). The second is a set of arrangements similar to the first, save that the state carries out, through tax policies and transfer payments, a redistribution whose effect is very much to narrow the inequalities of distribution, somewhat reducing total output and diminishing the rate of profit, but leaving

[62] If I understand him correctly, Barber is making very much the same point in a rather more precise and technically specific way. See Barber, "Justifying Justice," pp. 301ff.

corporate capitalism untouched, while improving the lot of the worst off. The third is a democratic socialist state that takes control (and "ownership") of the major concentrations of capital, producing thereby an income distribution much like that of the second (the added inequality of wealth distribution in the second set of arrangements might be offset by a larger spread in the income structure of the third).

These three sets of social arrangements will, in the model constructed by Rawls's theory, be three points on a social indifference map. The second and third will be preferred to the first, by virtue of the relative condition of the least advantaged representative man in each, and, as I have described them, the second and third will be roughly indifferent (or, to put it grammatically, the society will be indifferent when asked to choose between the second and the third).

But any model that portrays the second and third sets of arrangements as "close" to one another will be of no use at all in evaluating alternative societies or deciding in what direction to set out from our present condition. The political power of corporate capitalism will stand in the way of significant redistributions of income, unless some way can be found to protect the profit position of the corporations, either by extracting a surplus from abroad during a time of favorable trade or else by forcing the burden of redistribution onto the politically unorganized and ineffective sectors of the middle income brackets of the economy (such as small business or non-unionized workers, who suffer a real decline in income through inflation and stagnant wage levels). The democratic socialist alternative will, of course, appear far more difficult to reach, on first examination, but by making explicit the real shifts in economic power that are required, we may lay to rest the myth that income redistribution can be achieved painlessly, cooperatively, harmoniously, and within the present framework of private enterprise.

(Another way to get at the source of the inadequacy of Rawls's theory is to return to a point touched on earlier, namely Rawls's failure to focus squarely on the structure of *production* in the economy rather than on alternative patterns of *distribution*.) There is a deep ambivalence in Rawls's thought, running through his characterization of the bargaining game, his analysis of the difference principle, and even his moral psychology. On the one hand, as we have already seen, Rawls erects his entire theory on the notion of an inequality surplus, which requires some conception of the way in which goods and services are produced and even—rudimentarily—of the social relationships into which workers enter in the activity of production. On the other hand, the notion of a bargaining game, particularly of a game of fair division, treats the goods to be distributed as exogenously given. So far as the theory of games of fair division is concerned, no difference exists between dividing a pie that one or another of the players has baked and dividing a pie that has drifted gently down from the sky. That is what Nozick means when he alludes to "manna from heaven." The economic models employed by Rawls exhibit the same concern with distribution to the exclusion of production. Nothing in the notion of Pareto optimality, or in the formalism of an indifference map, requires us to distinguish between the ongoing distribution of goods and services produced in the daily reproduction of social life, and the parceling out of free gifts miraculously come upon. Welfare economics, we might say, is the pure theory of the cargo cult.

Not even the full panoply of neo-classical economics, with its theories of marginal productivity, its production functions, and its theorems of general equilibrium, tells us anything about the ways in which the organization of production determines the distribution of power and thereby establishes systematic patterns of exploitation and domination. Rawls does not deny the reality of political power, nor does he claim that it has its roots elsewhere than in the economic arrangements of a society. But by employing the models of analysis of the classical liberal tradition and of neo-classical economics, he excludes that reality from the pages of his book. Precisely because he has inflated his exposition enormously in pursuit of systematic wholeness, the absence has the effect of a denial, with consequences that are not merely false but ideological.

And yet, Rawls is ambivalent, as I have said. Nowhere is that ambivalence clearer than in his accounts, both explicit and implicit, of human motivation. As is by now well-known and understood, classical liberal economic and political theory—and with it the formal models of game theory and welfare economics—presuppose that human beings are utility-maximizers, seekers after gratification whose reason is employed in finding the most efficient allocation of their scarce resources. None of the psychological agnosticism of the axiomatic treatments of utility by von Neumann and Morgenstern and others can conceal the direct line from the simple egoistic hedonism of Bentham to the sophisticated utility functions of game theory and the indifference maps of ordinalist welfare economics. By employing those models of analysis, Rawls buys into their underlying psychological presuppositions.

Standing against the liberal-utilitarian conception of human nature is a much older tradition, going back to Aristotle and finding its most powerful expression in the writings of the young Marx, according to which creative,

208

productive, rational *activity* is the good for man. Consumption is essential to life; its gratifications form a component of the good life when properly integrated into a healthy and well-ordered psyche. But consumption is not, and cannot be, the end for man. For Marx (though not, save with regard to the intellect, for Aristotle), labor of the right sort is an indispensable element of the good life. To treat any expenditure of effort in labor time as a cost is a sign not of prudential rationality but of a warped and distorted personality. If all the labor available in a society can properly be treated as a disutility by workers, that can only be viewed as a sign that the natural productive activities of human beings have been distorted in ways destructive of true human happiness.

Now the strange thing is that Rawls more or less endorses this Aristotelian-Marxist conception of human nature! He even invokes Aristotle's name and sets in the center of his theory of the good a psychological thesis that he dubs the "Aristotelian Principle" (p. 426). The particular role of this principle in the theory is to justify certain orderings of bundles of primary goods from the standpoint of the original position, and we need not go into its details. But it is clear that Rawls does not think of himself as endorsing some modern-day version of the psychological hedonism of utilitarianism—very far from it.

I return thus to the point from which I began my analysis of Rawls's philosophy. At the heart of the theory in *A Theory of Justice* lies a formal model of a bargaining game. The power of the theory consists in the creativity and imagination of that device, by means of which Rawls hoped to bypass the sterile dispute between intuitionism and utilitarianism. Speaking narrowly, from within the framework of Rawls's own mode of analysis, the maneuver will not work because the model must either im-

209

pute too much particularity to the players, in order to enable them to bargain to a determinate and predictable outcome or else so totally strip them of their individuating characteristics that no determinate bargaining game can be defined.)

Looked at more broadly, however, Rawls's failure grows naturally and inevitably out of his uncritical acceptance of the socio-political presuppositions and associated modes of analysis of classical and neo-classical liberal political economy. By focusing exclusively on distribution rather than on production, Rawls obscures the real roots of that distribution. As Marx says in his *Critique of the Gotha Program*, "Any distribution whatever of the means of consumption is only a consequence of the distribution of the conditions of production themselves. The latter distribution, however, is a feature of the mode of production itself."

Is Rawls right? Because his two principles of justice abstract from the real foundations of any social and economic order, the question has no useful answer. Has Rawls sought the principles of justice in the right way? No, for his theory, however qualified and complicated, is in the end a theory of pure distribution. Rawls's enormous sophistication and imaginativeness shows us that the failure is due not to any inadequacies of execution, but rather to the inherent weaknesses of that entire tradition of political philosophy of which *A Theory of Justice* is perhaps the most distinguished product.

Bibliography

A *Theory of Justice* is the only book Rawls has published (Belknap Press of Harvard University Press, 1971). The dozen or so essays he has published in scholarly journals all deal with one or another aspect of the subject of that book. A bibliography of Rawls's works, and of articles on Rawls, up through early 1974, can be found in the special issue of *Social Theory and Practice*, Vol. 3, No. 1 (Spring, 1974), which is devoted to *A Theory of Justice*. That issue contains Andrew Levine's essay, "Rawls' Kantianism," to which I refer in Part Three of this essay, as well as several other interesting essays.

Reading Rawls: Critical Studies of A Theory of Justice, edited by Norman Daniels (Basic Books, 1974), also contains a bibliography of articles on Rawls, somewhat fuller and more up to date than that in *Social Theory and Practice*. Among the many interesting essays in Daniels's book, several of which have been cited in footnotes here, are those by Thomas Nagel, Ronald Dworkin, Gerald Dworkin, T. M. Scanlon, H.L.A. Hart, and Benjamin Barber.

The only other book-length treatment of Rawls's theory, to the best of my knowledge, is the widely read work by Brian Barry, *The Liberal Theory of Justice: A Critical Examination of the Principal Doctrines in* A Theory of Justice *by John Rawls* (Oxford, 1973). Barry's approach is rather different from mine, but I would hope that interested readers could find much to use and reflect on in both his essay and mine.

In response to this flood of comment on a book scarcely half a decade old, Rawls has started to "answer his critics." In addition to the essay, "Fairness to Goodness," in the *Philosophical Review*, referred to in a footnote, see "Reply to Alexander and Musgrave," *Quarterly Journal of Economics*, 88 (Nov. 1974), pp. 633–55.

211

BIBLIOGRAPHY

One of the marks of Rawls's importance as a political philosopher is the unusual extent to which scholars in fields other than philosophy have begun to comment on his theory. In addition to the essays by Harsanyi, Rae, and others from the *American Political Science Review* for June 1975, I have found especially suggestive several articles by Professor Hal R. Varian of the M.I.T. Economics Department. See, for example, "Equity, Envy, and Efficiency," in *Journal of Economic Theory*, Vol. 9, No. 1 (Sept. 1974), pp. 63–91.

But it is impossible to keep up with the literature on Rawls! As I write these last words, there arrives in the mail an advertisement for a new journal, *Midwest Studies in Philosophy*, whose first volume, for February 1976, announces essays by Homer E. Mason, Bernard Baumrin, and Virginia Held on topics directly relevant both to the particular concerns of this book and, more widely, to the study of Rawls's philosophy. I leave it to the author of the next book on Rawls to bring the bibliography up to date.

Index

213

LIBRARY OF CONGRESS CATALOGING IN PUBLICATION DATA

Wolff, Robert Paul.
  Understanding Rawls.

  Bibliography: p.
  Includes index.
  1. Rawls, John, 1921-   A theory of justice.
2. Justice.   I. Title.
JC578.R383W64   340.1'1   76-49527
ISBN 0-691-01992-4